Jay Wolke

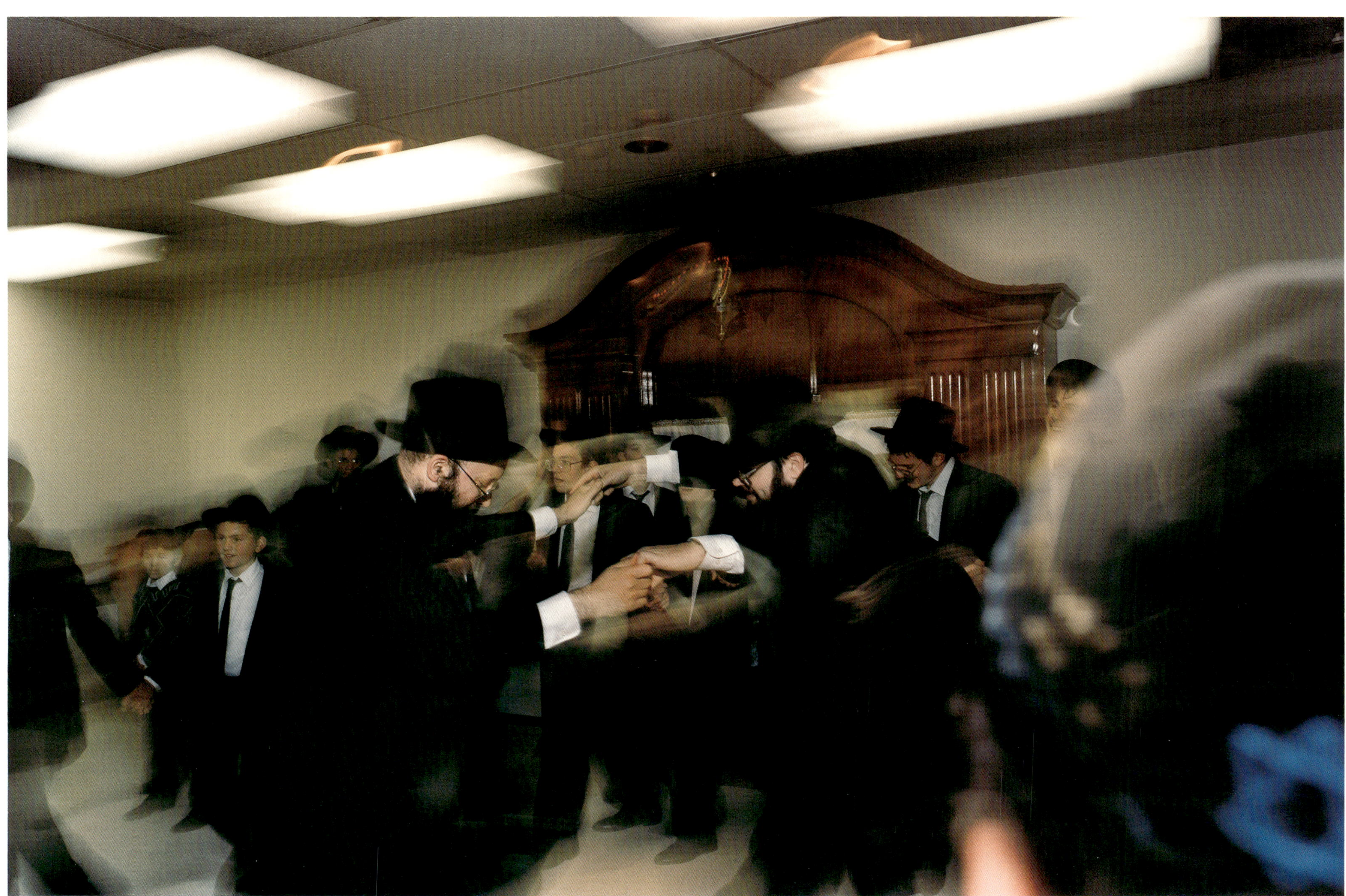

Jay Wolke

All Around the House

Photographs of American-Jewish Communal Life

With an essay by Joel Snyder

The Art Institute of Chicago

This book was published in conjunction with the exhibition "All Around the House: Photographs of American-Jewish Communal Life," organized by The Art Institute of Chicago and presented from May 23 to September 13, 1998.

Partial support for this project has been provided by the National Endowment for the Arts/Midwest Arts Alliance.

First Edition
Printed in the U.S.A.

Published by The Art Institute of Chicago, 111 South Michigan Avenue, Chicago, Illinois 60603-6110

Distributed worldwide by D.A.P./ Distributed Art Publishers, 155 Sixth Avenue, 2nd Floor, New York, N.Y. 10013-1507
Telephone: (212) 627-1999
Fax: (212) 627-9484

Edited by Michael Sittenfeld, Associate Editor of Publications

Production by Amanda W. Freymann, Associate Director of Publications—Production

Designed and typeset by Sam Silvio, Chicago

Color separations by Professional Graphics, Inc., Rockford, Illinois

Printed by Meridian Printing, East Greenwich, Rhode Island

Bound by Acme Bookbinding Company, Charlestown, Massachusetts

COVER:
Boxers, Whitney's Bat Mitzvah, Kenilworth, Illinois, 1994 (detail; see PL. 26)

FRONTISPIECE:
Men Dancing, Sukkoth Celebration, Yeshiva Migdal Torah, Chicago, 1993

Library of Congress Catalog Card Number: 98-070861

ISBN 0-86559-165-2

This book is dedicated to the memory of Estelle Wolke.

Contents

Preface

David Travis

Curator of Photography
The Art Institute of Chicago

The Psalmists sing "show me your ways," and the phrase echoes down the centuries through the Christian faithful and finds voice again in the Sephardic poet, Judah Halevi. As apt as such a phrase might have been for a book of photographs of Jewish culture, Jay Wolke's temperament is not so formally reverential. His own title, "All Around the House," favoring the spontaneous and inquisitive aspects of his photographic imagination, is a better description of the way he has approached his subject. Behind the levity of his title, however, is a quest for understanding timeless mysteries of the most profound kind. Part of what Wolke has learned resides within him and part is given back to us in his photographs. But, just as it is hard to learn, it is also hard to have what one has learned accepted.

It is easy to see that photographers like Wolke create pictures that are a pleasure for the eyes. Being artistically attractive, however, does not save his work from being a potential exasperation for those whose studied opinions form the extremes of Jewish religious thought. No single photographer's views could, of course, conform to the orthodoxy or the liberalism of those for whom the history of Jewish law, ritual, and culture are subjects of immense passion. That was not Wolke's goal.

Wolke's goal was to learn by question and observation and to teach by asking others to question his pictures. We may ask of the relevance of the photograph of the chubby-faced baby being tenderly pinched by an admirer. If pressed for a meaning, Wolke points to the median furrow we see over the baby's upper lip. That is where, it is said, an angel touched the child. For according to Jewish myth, before birth we know everything about the universe, but before entering the world an angel wipes away all memory with the stroke of a finger. Charming, but also not far removed from either Platonic philosophy or Wordsworth's Romantic ideas of our celestial origin in "Ode: Intimations of Immortality."

Wolke's photographs mean something first to him and then to us because they are the result of a personal voyage of discovery he began when nearing forty. Although initiated by two Jewish patrons of his photography, his pictures of Jewish culture in Chicago-area communities went beyond their commission. By making these photographs, Wolke came to terms with his family heritage and his own life as a photographer in postmodernist America. His father had immigrated to the United States from Poland, and became a national leader in the cause of Conservative Judaism. As a photographer, Wolke extended his father's mission of adapting the tradition of Jewish law and custom to new environments by stirring up the question of what is missed and what is gained by both the resistance and accommodation of Jewish traditions to contemporary society. But, searching for one's identity through one's family heritage is something thousands upon thousands of sons and daughters do. In Wolke's case, however, another equally ancient pursuit accompanied this age-old quest.

The desire to make something beautiful from what is revered, as the Psalmists demonstrated centuries ago, stimulates another kind of reflection upon how truth is both perceived and cherished. As truth comes differently to the ear in song than in lecture, so, too, does it address the eye with another mission as a picture than as a text. Thus, photographs enter and exit Wolke's personal editing process for what would seem to be arbitrary reasons. The fact that he uses six different kinds of color film and laboriously processes his own prints points to the value he places on color rendition and balance. The fact that he uses both a 6-by-7-cm and a 6-by-9-cm rangefinder camera points to the value that he places on exacting compositions. Color, composition, and the normal welter of extraneous elements not only make for the predicament of photographic choice of moment and point of view, but also symbolize the complexities of the subjects.

In Wolke's earlier work, he improvised on secular objects. From 1982 to 1985, he documented Chicago's Dan Ryan Expressway as it cut a swath through the South Side on its way to the fringe suburbs. Along this metropolitan incision, Wolke found everything from the makeshift habitats of the homeless to runners participating in well-advertised civic marathons. The highway's engineering or its planned traffic patterns were not the focus of his study. Rather he sought to discover the unexpected juxtapositions it made with the fabric of the city. His photographs of Las Vegas and Atlantic City, taken from 1987 to 1992, similarly avoided the obvious activity of gambling in an effort to depict the scenes and spectacles that surrounded it, the incidentals that, in fact, give these cities their character. Commentary on that which surrounds an assumed core and the resulting symbolism it provides is a strength that Wolke has found to be paramount in his chosen medium.

In many ways, Wolke's previous themes helped to prepare him for his observation of Jewish culture. But there were and remain substantial obstacles. For instance, very little in the sacred texts of the Torah suggests the kind of virtues that we celebrate in Wolke's photographs or in his attitude toward his subjects. Exodus and the other books of Moses offer little other than the well-worn phrase "stranger in a strange land" as a rubric. A few more possibilities reside in the poetic and wisdom books, but not many. Photographs melding melodrama, playfulness, and a requisite portion of contemporary irony rarely lend themselves to biblical parallels. Beyond that, photographs must deal primarily with surfaces, appearances, and illusions. Thus, photography is, from the outset, associated with the very qualities opposed by the traditional philosophic and theological approaches to scripture and ethics.

If the assumed core of Jewish law and history, that elusive center of unification, is purposely undepicted in Wolke's photographs, it is because the subject itself is both visually unobservable and historically unattainable. In addition, Wolke's habit of dealing with other assumed cores had proved to him that he works best when his approach is oblique. Through this approach, which is typical of most personal and documentary photographic projects, Wolke is able to address a subject well guarded by scholars. It is a method that allows him to mix charm with provocation, a combination for which most contemporary artists, as well as enlightened teachers, actively strive.

Because Wolke has come to enjoy dealing with paradox, or at least with odd juxtapositions, one could relate his work to that of any number of other contemporary artists. But Wolke's photographs have a unique and a surprising kinship with something entirely different. His work finds a happy companionship with the delightful stories of Jewish folklore or certain books of the Talmud that attempt to discover meaning other than the literal ones of the Torah. In what have been called puzzle stories and wisdom tales of this literature, the main character, like a photographer, is required to make an instantaneous decision in facing a seemingly unresolvable predicament. Sometimes the writer creates a humorous solution and sometimes a profound one in revealing the truth underlying the tale.

One famous story from this literature, whose source is in a book of the Talmud called *Pirkei Avot* (*Sayings of the Fathers*), can be aptly paired with Wolke's attitude. That is, it can be paired with the photographer's understanding that what seems just outside any core is not only what resists or accommodates itself to foreign environments but what is often the only thing available for the photographer to examine and comment upon. The story concerns Hillel the Elder, a learned Pharisee of the period of the Second Temple (first century B.C.E.), who is one of the most respected and beloved rabbis of a very long history.

Rabbi Hillel was known for his patience as much as his insight. In one folktale version of the story, this trait provided a target for a courtier from King Herod's palace who made a wager with his friends that he could make the great teacher angry. For several days, the courtier disrupted the study house with strange and irrelevant questions. Hillel responded instantly with terse answers appropriate to the questions and then went on, unperturbed, with his lessons. Finally, in exasperation, the courtier zeroed in on the core of Jewish law and history, and asked a ridiculous yet challenging question. It brought him the attention of the assembled students who had spent years in study. The courtier asked the wise scholar if he could say the whole of what Torah teaches while standing on one foot. Raising one foot, and with it the weight of centuries of study and exegesis, Hillel looked at his tormentor and responded, "That which is hateful unto yourself, do it not unto your neighbor." It was a splendid answer, as ever.

Of course, there was much more and Hillel knew it. That his answer had a meaning wrung from his paraphrasing of Leviticus 19:18 signaled that he felt more than the ancient core had become essential. In character with his brilliance, the sentences that followed his famous answer were equally terse and shocking. In them one can discern his wit from the slight twist of irony compatible with many of Wolke's photographs.

Before sage Hillel put his foot down he added, "That is the whole of Torah. The rest is commentary. Now go and learn."

Vos Macht a Yid?

Joel Snyder

Professor, Department of Art History
University of Chicago

We, even those of us who happen to be Jewish, come to many of Jay Wolke's photographs as outsiders of one kind or another.[1] If Wolke's photographs show us that a Jewish life is always lived within a community and is necessarily inhabited, so to speak, out in the open, what he also shows is how unlike Jewish communities are from one another and how important these differences can be. This has always been true—in ancient times, for example, Hellenized Jews differed from those who refused the culture of Greece; and Jewish sects during the Roman occupation of Judea established differences among themselves and were distinct, in certain respects, from the Orthodoxy centered in Jerusalem—and the Orthodoxy in the capital was itself factionalized.

The history of the Jews is one of repeated exile, dispersal, and in certain crucial respects, accommodation to the local practices of indigenous cultures. Religious Jews in diaspora have ruled themselves according to rabbinical law, devising at the same time their own distinct ways of staying true to the religion and culture of Israel. The great separation of Jews into the Mediterranean Sephardim and the Northern and Eastern European Ashkenazim continues to this day, although in attenuated and changing forms owing to continuous emigration and immigration. The dizzying proliferation of separate and partially separated cultural communities is further embodied today, especially in America, in the differences between the religious and attendant practices of Orthodox, Conservative, Reform, and Reconstructionist Jews. Accordingly, it has rarely been easy for a Jew to say, with any hope of being precise, what constitutes being Jewish, although it has been, at times, far too easy for non-Jews to provide, if not a definition, then some sort of indubitable test of supposedly ineradicable Jewishness: bodily appearance (dark skin, hooked nose); blood; a preoccupation with money; a steadfast unwillingness, or an inherent incapacity, to be like "everybody else."

The United States has provided an extraordinary medium for Jewish life. Free from the threat of pogroms and organized state hostility—if not entirely unencumbered by informal, stubborn patterns of refined exclusion and discrimination that have flared up at times into criminal acts—Jewish communities have thrived here. The initial and relatively small immigration of Sephardic and then Central European Jews of the seventeenth and eighteenth centuries to America was followed in the late nineteenth and twentieth centuries by a major influx of primarily, but not exclusively, Eastern European immigrants, many of whom did not come here for abstract reasons that might be captured in a word like "freedom"—most were merely reenacting the ancient Jewish tragedy of making an exodus from oppression. Though these immigrants may have come to escape the terrors and humiliations of living elsewhere, they, their children, and their grandchildren learned some American lessons quickly—learned something about the culture of America and in so doing, helped transform it. These immigrants and those who followed have had an enormous impact on American life—in commerce, medicine, the arts and sciences, entertainment, teaching, in statecraft and philanthropy—in almost every space in which American life is lived. The achievements of Jews in America have been fluorescent, as if the millennia of dispersal, wandering, and the economic and political restraints placed upon them had bottled up an enormous and constantly building pressure that finally exploded in America, releasing the energies of countless gifted men and women: Emma Goldman, Albert Einstein, Aaron Copland, Jonas Salk, Hannah Arendt, George Gershwin, Cynthia Ozick, Helen Frankenthaler, Helen Levitt, Alfred Stieglitz, Paul Strand, Diane Arbus, Barnett Newman, Felix Frankfurter, and Ruth Bader Ginsburg. But for all the splendor of the achievements of these and so many others, there is an unhappy side to playing the name game—a downcast aspect to the seemingly playful delight many Jews take in rehearsing the accomplishments of other Jews. Naming names is not just like the pleasure taken by a committed fan of a victorious home team, which is very much a pleasure taken in being part of a community. Playing the name game is a pleasure, but it is also (and especially for middle-class and wealthy Jews in the context of life in America) a compulsion driven by the need to be recognized as having made a special contribution not merely to some local community, or city, or state, but somehow to the whole of America—perhaps even to the idea of America itself. Reciting names is a way of declaring that Jews have earned the right to be Americans, deserve to be part of the fabric of America—in virtue not merely, as we Americans put it, of having "paid their own way," but of having given back twice, or ten times, or a hundred times what others have contributed. This compulsion speaks from a real and only recently gained self-assurance that remains nonetheless embedded in ancient fears of being treated differently from others, of being seen as forever on the outside with no claim to the inside, the fear, that is, of being seen as "parasites" (as the Nazi propagandists put it) who only take, but never give back.

What I mean to emphasize here is something about the complexity of Jewish life in America because it is this tangle of habits and customs, impulses and energies that constitute the raw material of Jay Wolke's project. It is a complexity we all understand intuitively as Americans. What Jews have had to learn is that being an American involves a constant struggle to be the same as everyone else while simultaneously maintaining, insisting upon real differences—and learning, too, to accept this condition as basic to being an American of any kind. Authenticity in America is not a matter of always occupying the insider position. All Americans constantly reshuffle their positions as insiders and outsiders. Chicago is a city of neighborhoods—Irish, Polish, Hispanic, German, Jewish, African-American, and many others—it is nonetheless "Sweet Home, Chicago" to all of us despite the fact that there are spaces we occupy as insiders and those to which we must always come as outsiders. There is, then, an inevitable "us" and "other" in America, and we live our lives effortlessly applying these distinctions—city, regional, ethnic, religious—changing the range of "us" and "other" to fit the circumstances and identifying ourselves sometimes as "us," sometimes as "other."[2]

Jay Wolke's photographs center entirely on the various Jewish communities in and around Chicago. His pictures insist upon profound religious and cultural differences among Jews—at once describing in bold and often exquisite terms the varieties of Jewish patterns of living, dwelling on the ordinary and the amazing and at the same time defying a viewer's impulse to generalize from the evidence his pictures present. If Wolke's question is "What is it to be a Jew?" his impulse is to respond in Talmudic fashion: a good question begets—never an answer—but always a further question. His answer is a picture maker's answer: "What is a Jew? Why don't you look and see?"

The usual terms of photographic criticism are not terribly useful in helping to make sense not merely of Wolke's individual photographs, but of all his photographs in ensemble.

Of course Wolke's project is, in some sense, "documentary," but relying on this old workhorse of photographic criticism is not terribly helpful because it fails to provide specificity for his project. It serves no worthwhile purpose to think of Wolke's photographs as documenting the lives of some Jews in Chicago in the mid-1990s—this accomplishes no more than restating the obvious, but worse, it suggests that the photographs are illustrative, that they would work, for example, as elements in a 1950s *Life* magazine feature story, and this, it seems to me, is simply wrong. The photographs present no coherent narrative, there is no text they illustrate—they work, often in compelling ways, against coherence.

Again, the notion that these are "insider" photographs suggests that the photographer has had special permission to enter where many of us may not, and while it is clearly true that Wolke's photographs were made from positions within disparate communities, it has the unfortunate consequence of suggesting that they are views of exotic peoples, not unlike pictures from ancient issues of *National Geographic*. But these pictures are not at all akin to the popular ethnographic studies of the 1930s and 1940s, nor are they usefully compared to, say, the pictures of Jacob Riis, who portrayed the urban poor of New York City in the 1880s and 1890s (including a large community of Jewish immigrants) as if they were prisoners in some distant and exotic jungle archipelago, which just happened to be lower Manhattan. Finally, Wolke's photographs are not informed by a romantic impulse to record a vanishing culture (the impulse behind the native American photographs of Edward Sherif Curtis), or by the fearful sense of impending doom that drove Roman Vishniac to photograph the last days of *shtetl* life in Poland. His photographs refuse typical labels because the project is anything but typical.

Part of what is so arresting about many of Wolke's photographs is that the trappings of quite ordinary American consumer culture are everywhere in them—that even his most eye-catching and singular photographs of ancient rituals carry the indelible marks of everyday life in America and that the combination of the ordinary and the unfamiliar, shown in the particular way he shows them, is both jarring and disconcerting. Take, for example, the wry portrayal Wolke gives us of the most ancient of Jewish rituals, the *brit millah*, or circumcision of the eight-day-old infant (*Steve's Bris, Elijah's Chair* [PL. 7]), which God stipulates to Abraham in Genesis 17.11-12, as a mark of His covenant with the Jews. In Wolke's photograph, an older man places the infant on a sofa, atop a decorated blanket—the two together symbolizing the throne of the prophet Elijah. The elaborately decorated blanket is protected by a plastic cover, and the man who so tenderly places the child on Elijah's Chair—the infant's grandfather who participates in this sacred ceremony—carries a pager in his pocket. This man, who assists in reenacting the ancient "covenant in the flesh," comes armed with a device that keeps him constantly in touch with another world. The photograph does more than replay the tired commonplace of the old living alongside the new, it initmates the temptations of the new and the increasing difficulty, perhaps the impossibility in America, of keeping the sacred world wholly apart from the profane. Here, the consecrated cloth of the ritual is enfolded in the transparent, heavy-gauge plastic that is one of the hallmarks of middle American consumer culture and the pager, should it go off, will, with its incessant beeping, transport the proceedings from the realm of the sacred to the world of the ordinary and everyday.

Orthodox Jews (of whom the Hasidim constitute only one branch) are committed to notions of separation in every aspect of their lives: plates and utensils used for the serving of meat are kept apart from those used for dairy products; women and girls do not occupy the same part of the synagogue as men and boys; in social settings, men dance with men and women dance with women. Their laws forbidding the admixture of things that must be kept separate extend even to prohibitions against the combining of different types of thread in the production of cloth that will be fashioned into clothing. Many of Wolke's photographs of Orthodox Jews have the notion of separation as their subtexts, even when separation does not seem to be an issue at all. In *Burning Chometz Before Passover* (PL. 2), we see a crowd of men and boys in a typical Chicago back alley, disposing of *chometz*—food containing (or even suspected of containing) leaven—by burning it in large drums. Smoke engulfs the figures as a young boy pours Idahoan dried mashed potato flakes into the fire. This ritual takes place on the evening before the festival of Passover, as Orthodox kitchens and pantries are cleansed of all products that carry any trace of leaven and certain legumes. Passover is the celebration of the Israelite Exodus from Egypt, a time marked by the eating of matzo—bread made without leavening. Although the ritual of burning food tainted with leaven is an ancient one, Wolke so constructs the picture as to drive the viewer's eye to the package of potato flakes from which puffs of steam and smoke seem to emanate.

The spilling over of the sacred into the everyday of America comes up in surprising ways in Wolke's photographs. In the chaos of a ritual springtime celebration, a boy is caught forever in the joy of running (*Lag B'Omer Festival, Horwich J.C.C.* [PL. 20]). He wears a colorful T-shirt, emblazoned with the words "Moshiach Be Prepared!" Under the English, the word "Moshiach" is repeated in Hebrew. The word means "Messiah." In this American spring, in the time of the rebirth of the earth, the boy might wear a standard issue Bulls T-shirt, but in this community he advertises the coming of the end of days. In another photograph, we peer at the display in a window of an Orthodox religious articles shop on Devon Avenue (*Window, Chicago Hebrew Book Store* [PL. 62]). It is remarkable that among academics, Judaism is often and erroneously portrayed as an antipictorial, iconoclastic culture. The relation of Jewish practice to the use of pictures, statues—"graven" and ungraven images of all kinds—has always been complex. In the past few hundred years, the prohibition against making images has all but disappeared (although the restriction against worshipping them can never be lifted). Look into this window and note the profusion of pictures. Some of them are not merely pictures to put into albums, or hang on walls—they are children's trading cards bearing the images of great Orthodox rabbis, cards made in the image of baseball and football trading cards.

Many of Wolke's photographs attest to the ongoing process of remembering and bearing witness to the Holocaust, an overwhelming theme of middle-class Jewish life. In one of the most haunting photographs in the collection (PL. 53), a woman stands bolt upright in a mixed, seated congregation of men and women. They all await the beginning of a Holocaust lecture by Elie Wiesel. She stands for reasons we shall never know, a descendant of the history that unfolds behind her in the stained-glass windows.

These are photographs made for exhibition in a museum of art. They are meant to be seen in public, enlarged to 16 by 20 or 20 by 24 inches, and were not made to be viewed in private in the way that we look at photographs in books. They are pictures made for display in a community setting. The seriousness of their intention may seem to be undermined by the character of their presentation. Jay Wolke is an accomplished photographer whose work as a commercial picture maker is inseparable from his talent as a teacher of photography and his skill at making photographs for exhibition in a museum of art. The terms of museum display of photographs has changed over the past few decades, and the fashions of recent years have seen a shift from exhibition as a means of achieving intimacy between photograph and viewer in a subdued museum setting to a frankly spectacular mode of address between photograph and public.

Most of the photographs of Alfred Stieglitz, Paul Strand, Edward Weston, and Walker Evans, to name four of the most consistently interesting American modernist photographers of this century, are small—ranging from 2 by 3 inches to 8 by 10 inches—and as such require, even when shown in a museum, a closing of the distance between viewer and picture. Their pictures cannot be seen by many people at once—they must be viewed up-close, privately, though in a public setting. They must be approached by the viewer. Also, by being almost exclusively monochrome, they call attention to their age, but even more importantly, they advertise their detachment from the everyday, profane world of color snapshots and commercial illustration. A common thread that runs through the various theories of modernist photography, one might even say the theological core of photographic modernism, is a conception of the purity of its means and ends. To have aesthetic value, a photograph has to be "purely photographic," free of reference to work in other media, free of handwork, free of the taint of commerce. The verbal packaging—the rhetoric—into which modernist photography was set like a jewel, demanded a separation of pure photographs from all others, insisting on the autonomy, the self-sufficiency of unadulterated photographs. This division of photography into the realm of the pure and the domain of the impure was originally modeled on conceptions of the sacred and the profane drawn from religious practice. The role of the museum, as a temple to the muses, was to provide a sacred space for the display of pure, impeccable pictures.

Jay Wolke's photographs are made in a time in which the visual environment has changed radically and, with it, the practices of photographers and museums. We live in an age of the spectacle, a time in which the stakes of visual engagement are raised daily. We have learned to expect gargantuan and previously unimaginable visual delights in movie theaters and we have come to demand equivalent presentations from television—in recent years television screens have doubled and tripled in viewing area. We have come to expect these visual delights everywhere, even in sports arenas where video replays hype the game and the game, in turn, hypes the replays. Print and electronic media—magazines, journals, newspapers, billboards, the Internet—compete constantly for the attention of our eyes, addressing us as potential consumers of their wares. Nearly all feature films are now produced in color (only purists, or those seeking the delights of nostalgia, make films in black and white) and even the *New York Times* has surrendered to competitive pressures that have come to characterize the end of this century, adopting the use of front-page, four-color photographs. Wolke's choice of materials and format are embedded in this visual culture, referring to it constantly, and his response to omnipresent spectacles has been to work in a large format, with highly saturated colors—to become a master of colors that he makes present in his photographs, colors which generally go unnoticed or colors so thoroughly exaggerated that they bear little resemblance to those that were present in front of his camera. It would be critically perverse to insist that his photographs are *about* color, as if making him into a modernist-turned-inward-on-his-medium would give his work a kind of seriousness it otherwise might be thought incapable of possessing. The work is serious, if what that means is that it is worthy of being shown in a museum, but the terms of seriousness have changed. Museums of art have changed too.

Wolke is no photographic modernist. His typical mode of assembling the elements of his pictures—of composing and finishing them—is a hybridized procedure, a cross between commercial production and shooting home snapshots. Even when his subjects strike us as bizarre, the photographs retain a double kind of familiarity, one that is both perfectly and remarkably suited to his project. Wolke's photographs combine something of the intimacy of the snapshots we keep in our desk drawers with the easy familiarity, slickness, and craft of advertising illustration. In certain respects, his work is reminiscent of the pictures we see in plush consumer advertisements and motion pictures, with their carefully laid out and precise balancing of light to produce even illumination and their extraordinary use of color—especially lavishly saturated color. But home snapshots are meant to remind us of home, while advertising photographs are successful only to the extent that they put us into the mood to consume what they display—and they can do that only by attracting the eye, holding its attention, and more often than not, by promoting desire. If modernism as a movement in the visual arts depended on the centrality of the artistic medium and its use to transfigure the ordinary so that it could be resituated on the sacred walls of the museum, its aim was to introduce us to a world that was supposed to be available only from art and only in a museum, or in a space set aside to be museumlike. It is true that what Wolke presents to us in his photographs is available only from them and cannot be retrieved by going back to the places or re-creating the events they portray. To that extent, and only to that extent, they are continuous with modernist practice. But I am trying to draw attention to the profound change of address these pictures require. Wolke's photographs cannot be viewed as subsisting in a sacred domain—their magnified splendor, pumped-up color, glossy surfaces all play off two forms of the commonplace world that surrounds us—return us, that is, to the contexts from which they were derived—family snapshots and the hyped consumer marketplace. These photographs do not invite analysis as items of modernist delight—as autonomous objects from the ancient and timeless realm of the aesthetic. They are intimately tied to the endless visual flux of the spectacular present. Wolke's photographs force us to attend to the visual stuff that makes our environment postmodernist. They do so by permitting us a view of the complex culture of a people whose devotion to the past everywhere intersects with the anxieties and pressures and pleasures of the present.

Notes

1. "Vos macht a Yid?" is a Yiddish expression based on the German "Was machst du?"—a friendly greeting, much like the French "Comment ça va?" ("How goes it?"). However, "Vos macht a Yid?" asks more than "How are you?"—it addresses the question to a self-acknowledged Jew, by a greeter who identifies himself as a Jew. In other words, the question/greeting establishes a community.

2. I recently overheard a man and a woman whose forebears came to this country on the *Mayflower*—this was at a dinner party in Boston—making reference, sotto voce, to "PLUs." Informal research at Harvard revealed that the letters stand for "People Like Us." Even those who imagine themselves located at the core of American society need to have ways of separating and combining.

Plates

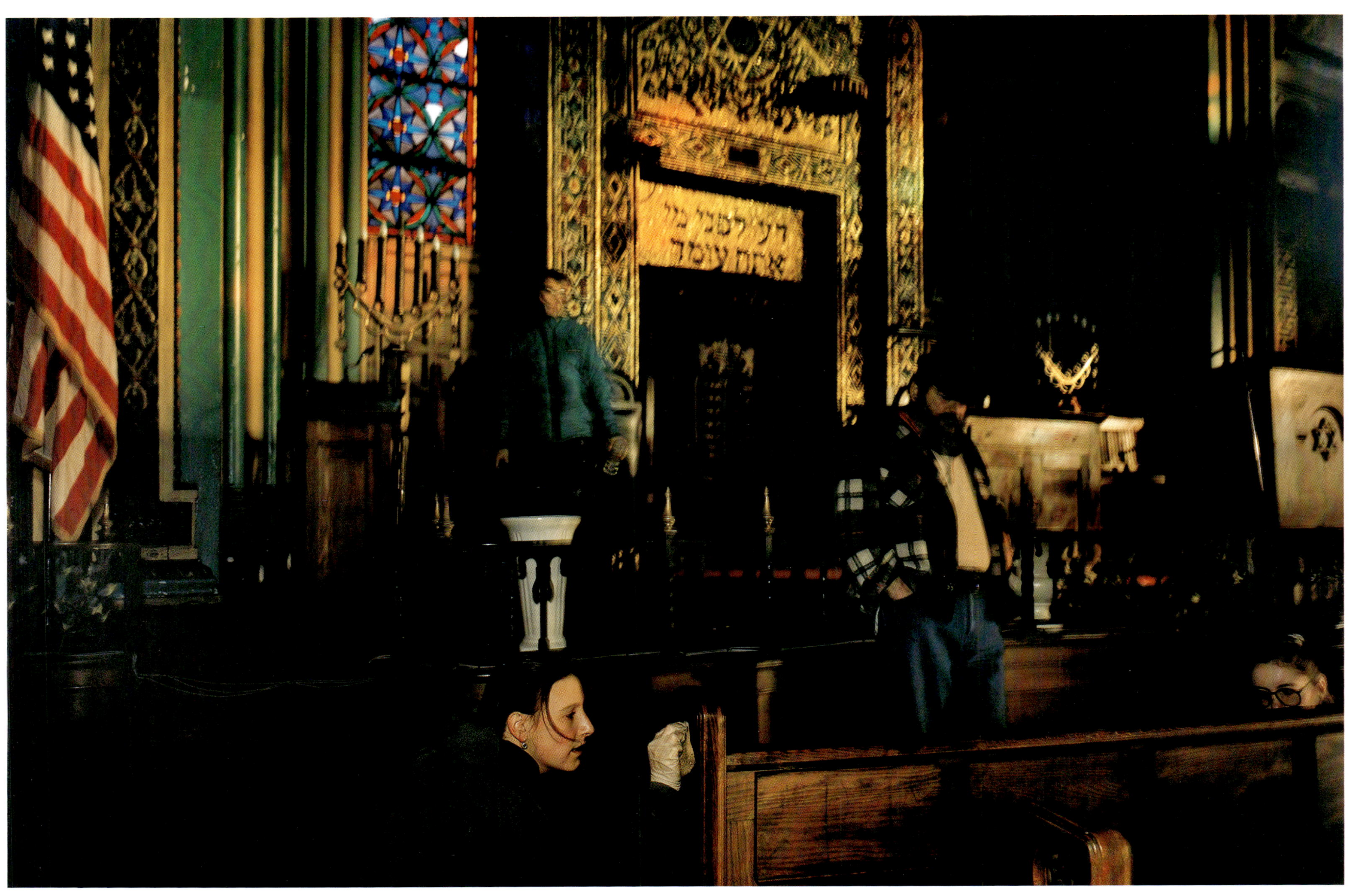

1 *Da Lifnei Mi Atah Omed (Know Before Whom You Stand), Sanctuary, Congregation Agudas Achim,* Chicago, 1994

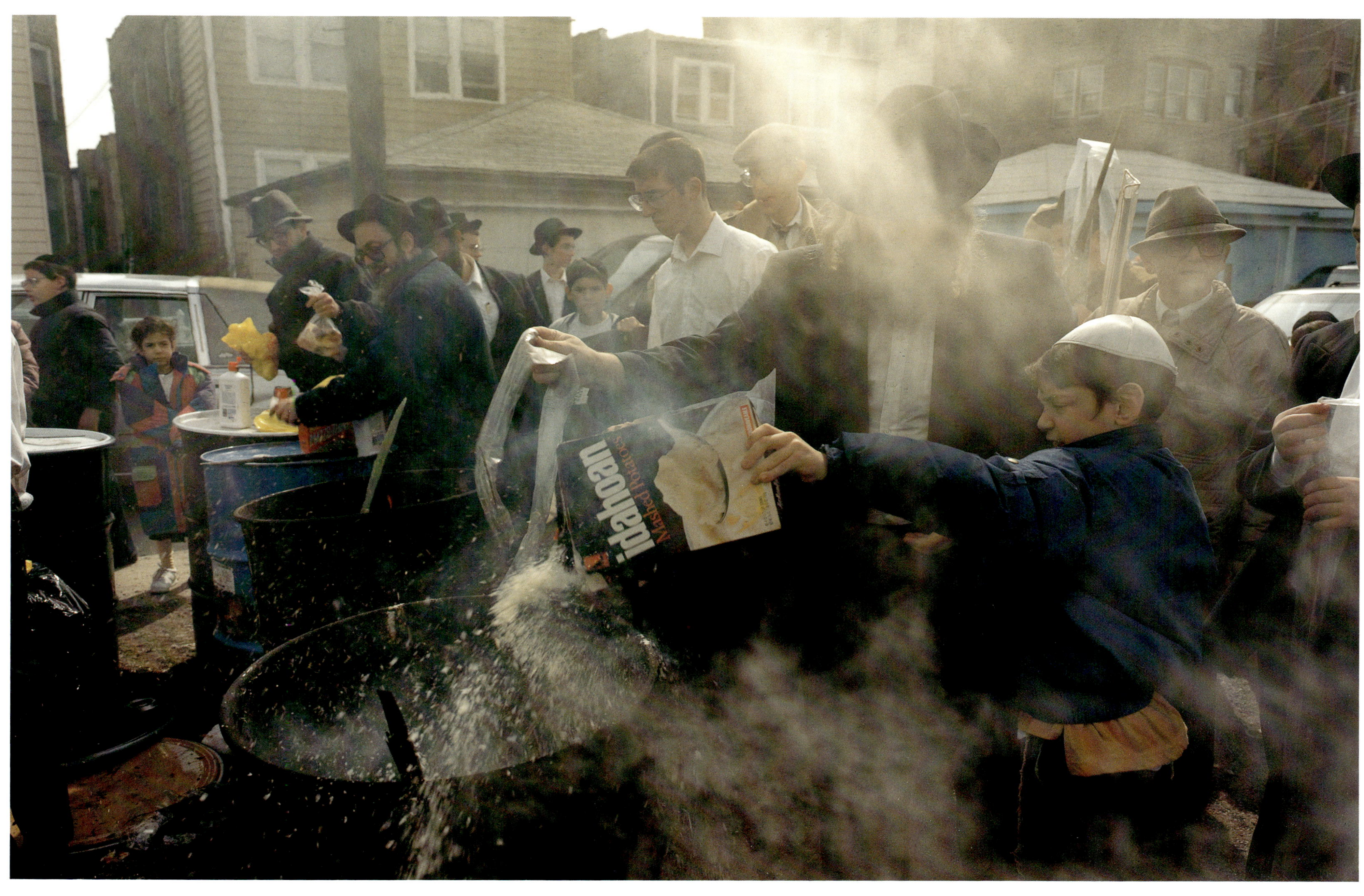

2 *Burning Chometz Before Passover,* Chicago, 1993

3 *Schlogging Kapporoth Before Yom Kippur,* Chicago, 1994

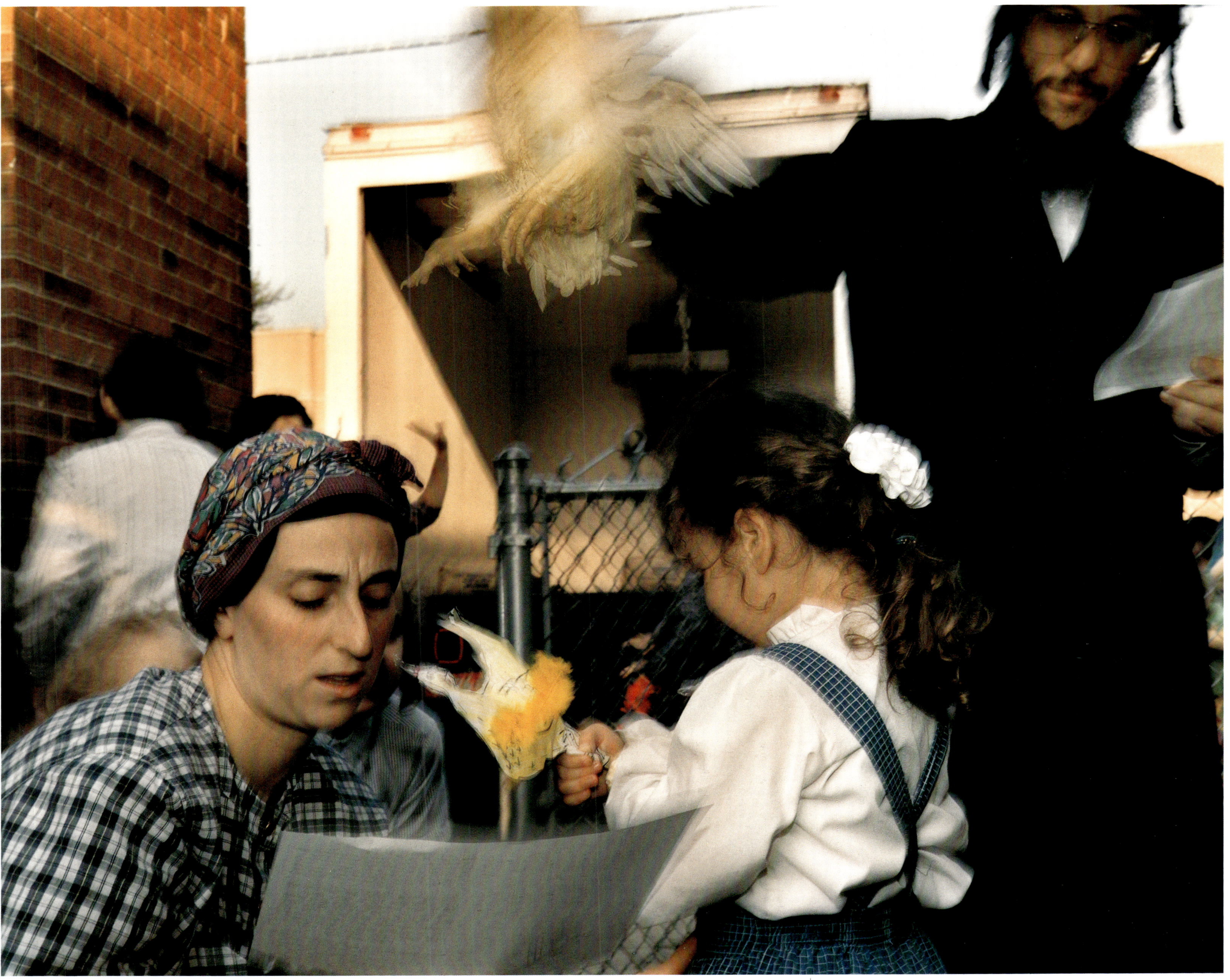

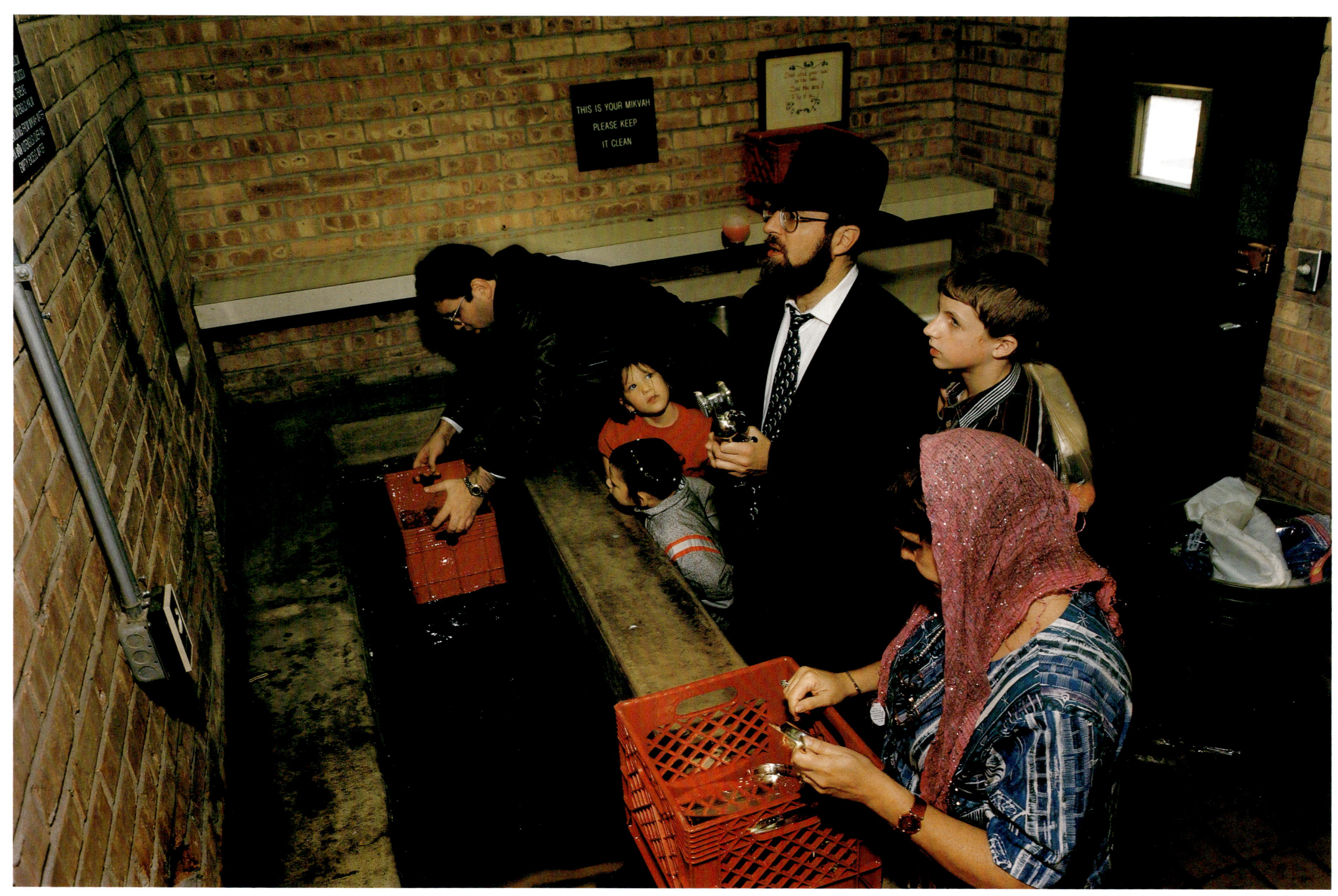

4 *Toyveling at the Mikvah,* Chicago, 1995

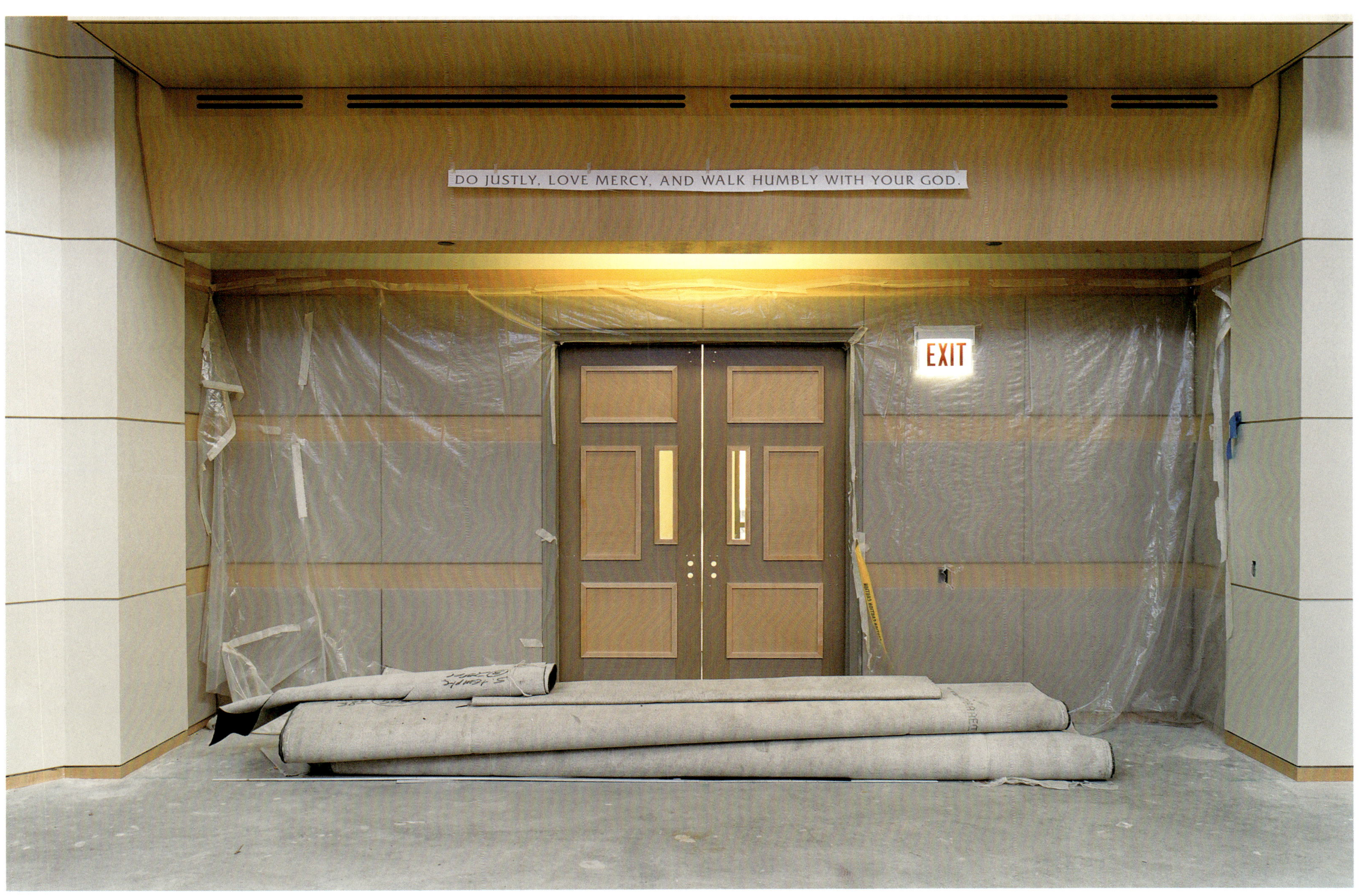

5 *Sanctuary Construction, Temple Sinai,* Chicago, 1994

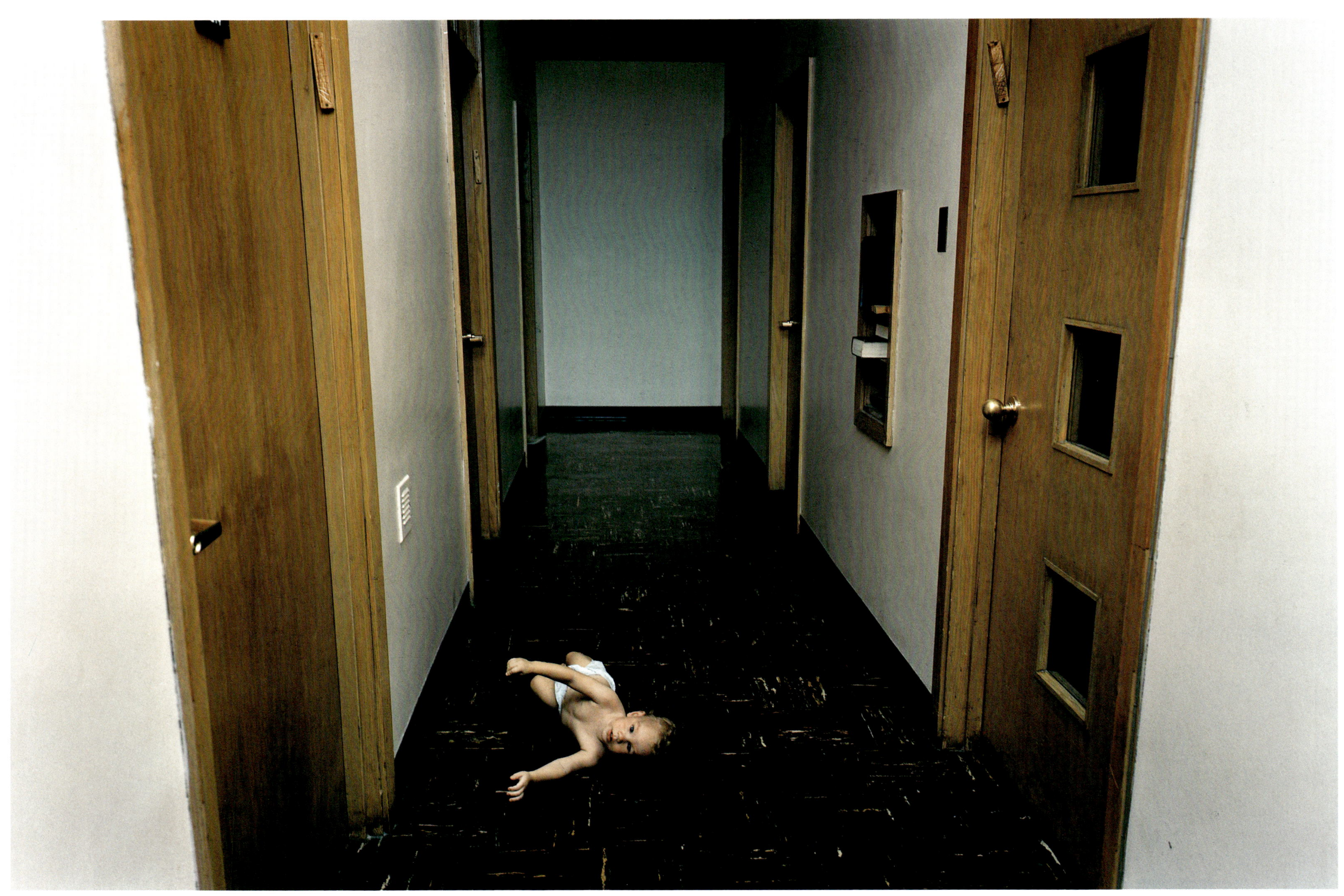

6 *Baby in Hallway, Jewish Homeless Shelter,* Chicago, 1994

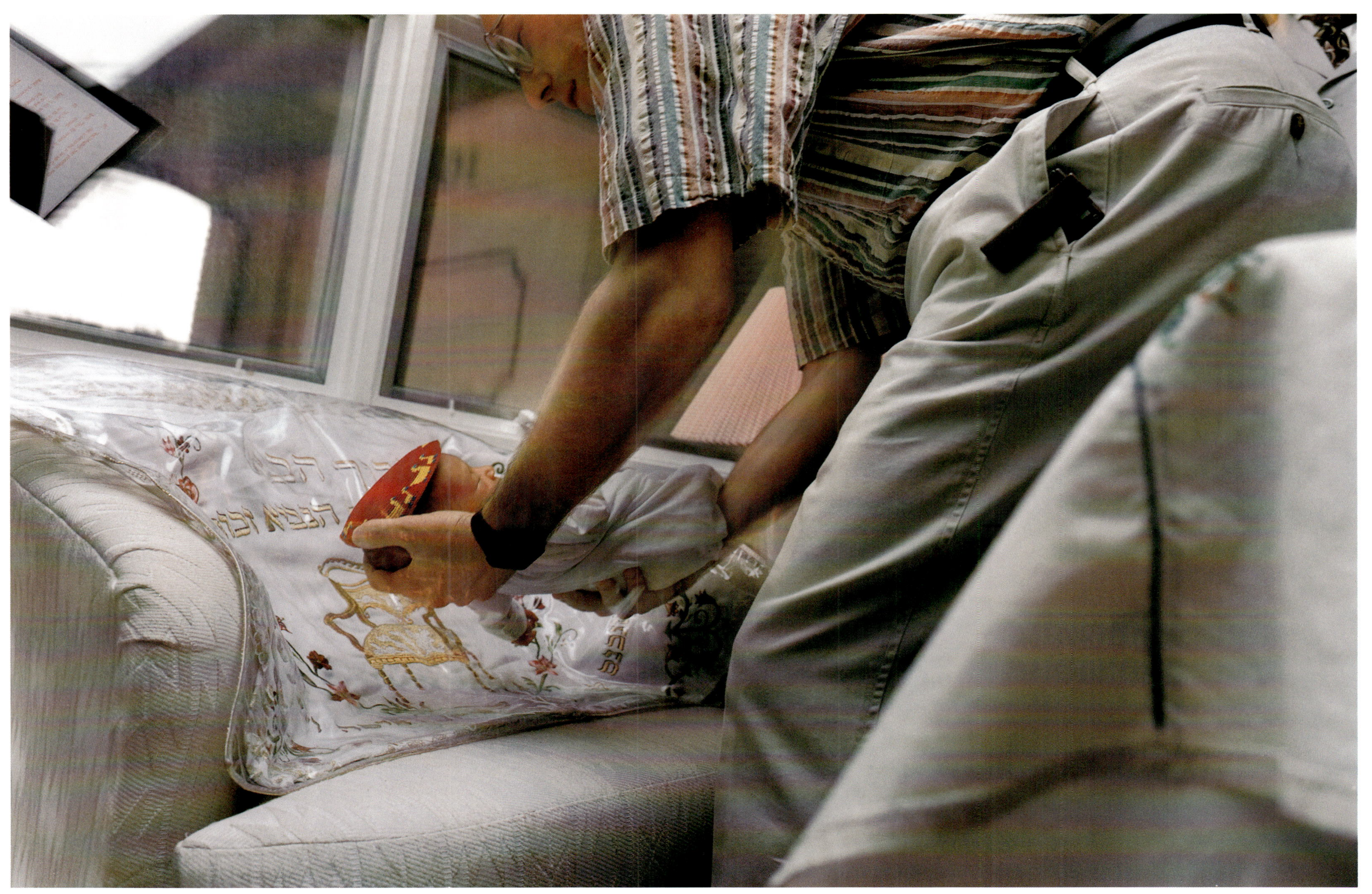

7 *Steve's Bris, Elijah's Chair,* Deerfield, Illinois, 1996

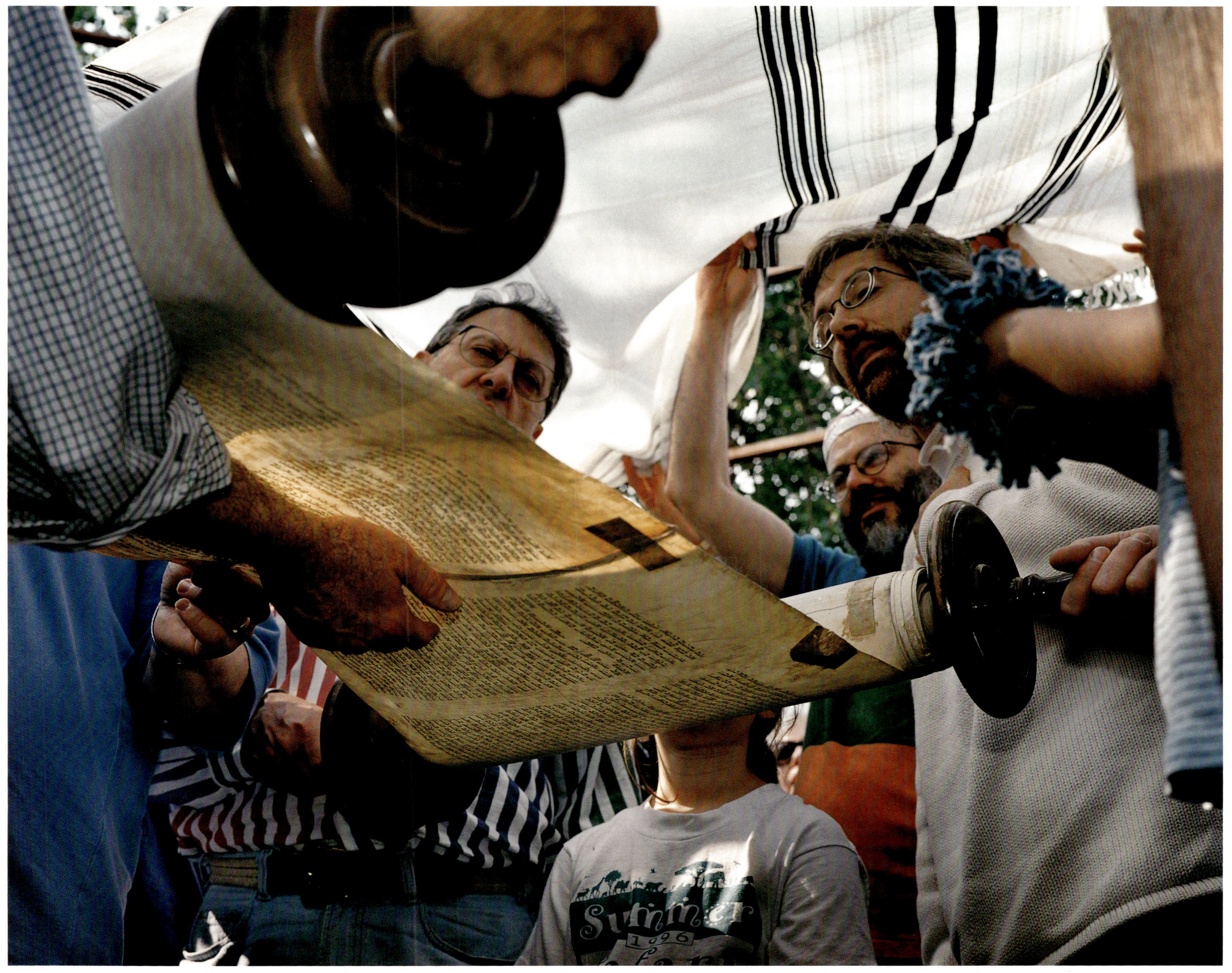

8 *Torah Reading, Shavuot, Congregation Etz Haim,* Camp Beber, Mukwonago, Wisconsin, 1997

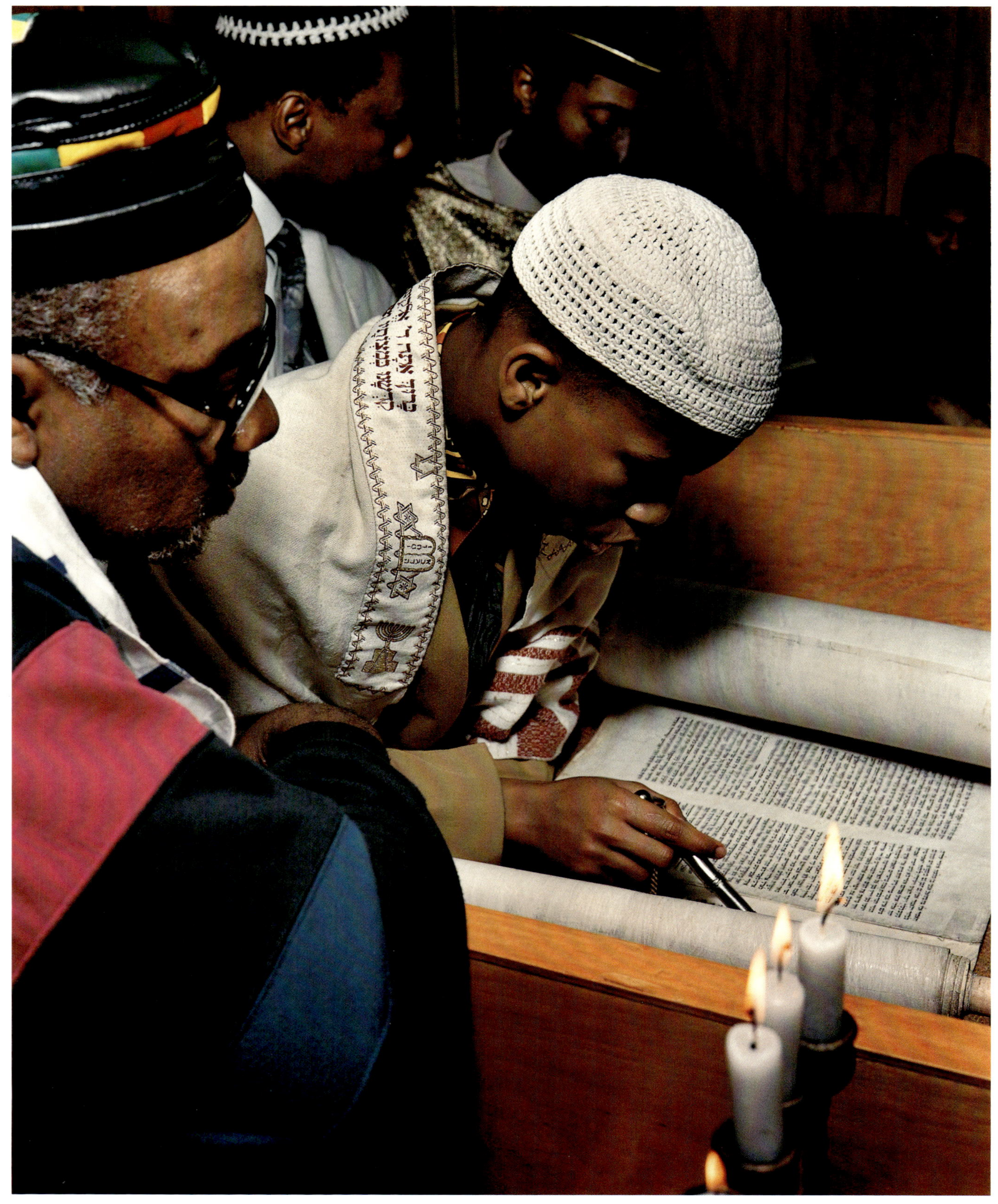

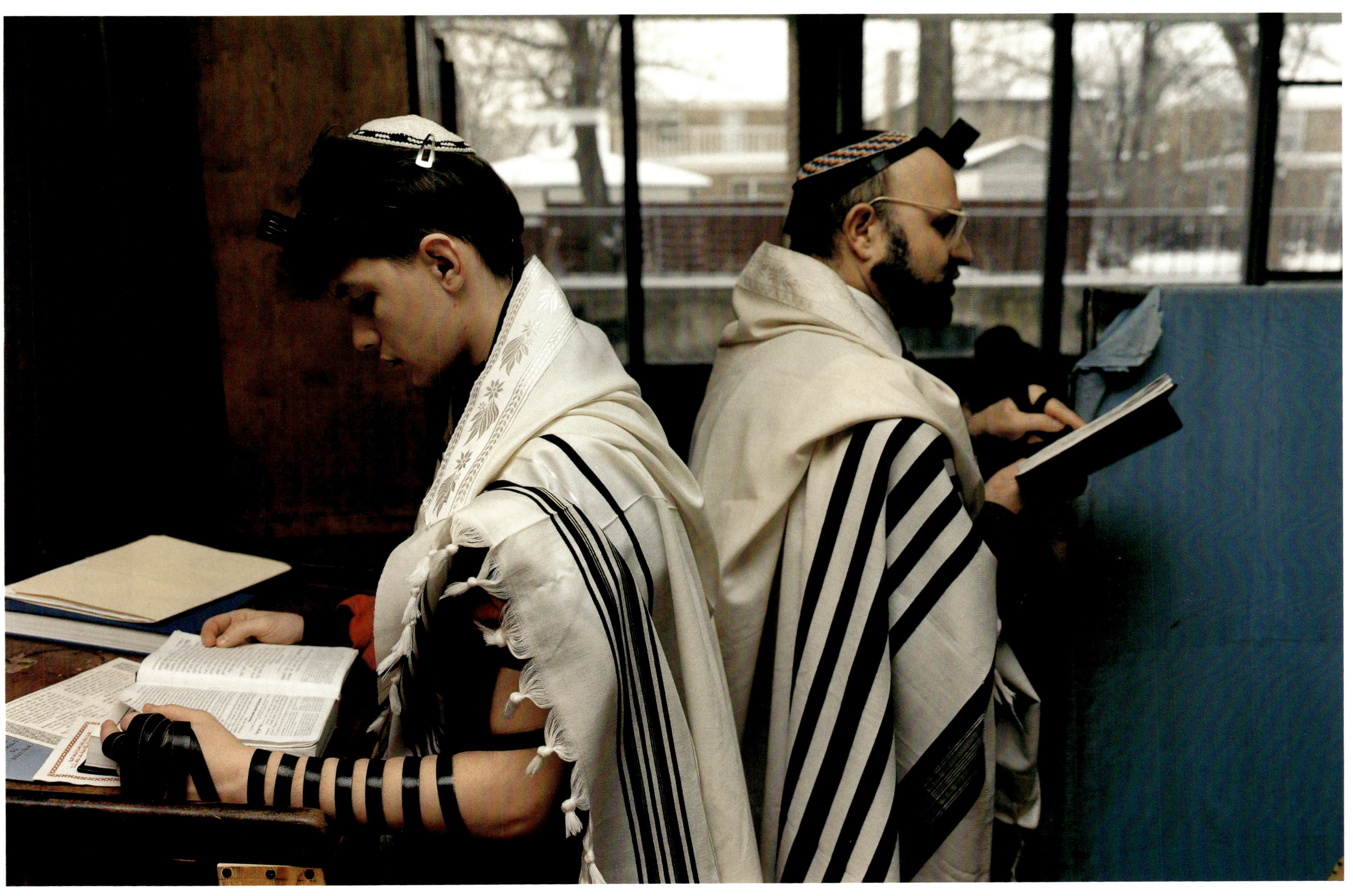

9 *Torah Reading, Beth Shalom B'Nai Zaken Ethiopien Congregation,* Chicago, 1994

10 *Boys, Morning Service, Ida Crown Academy,* Chicago, 1993

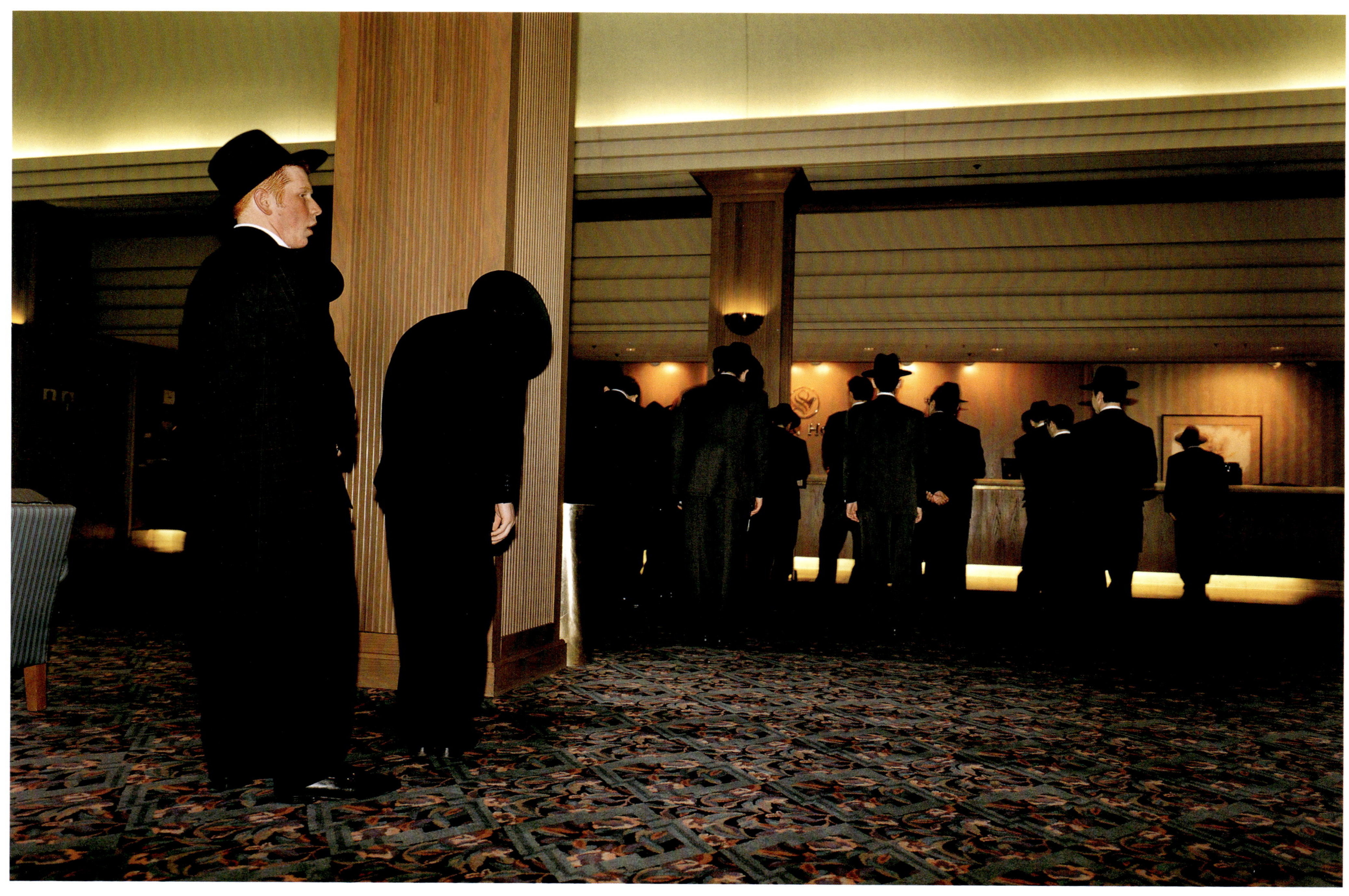

11 *Evening Service, Westin O'Hare Lobby,* Rosemont, Illinois, 1997

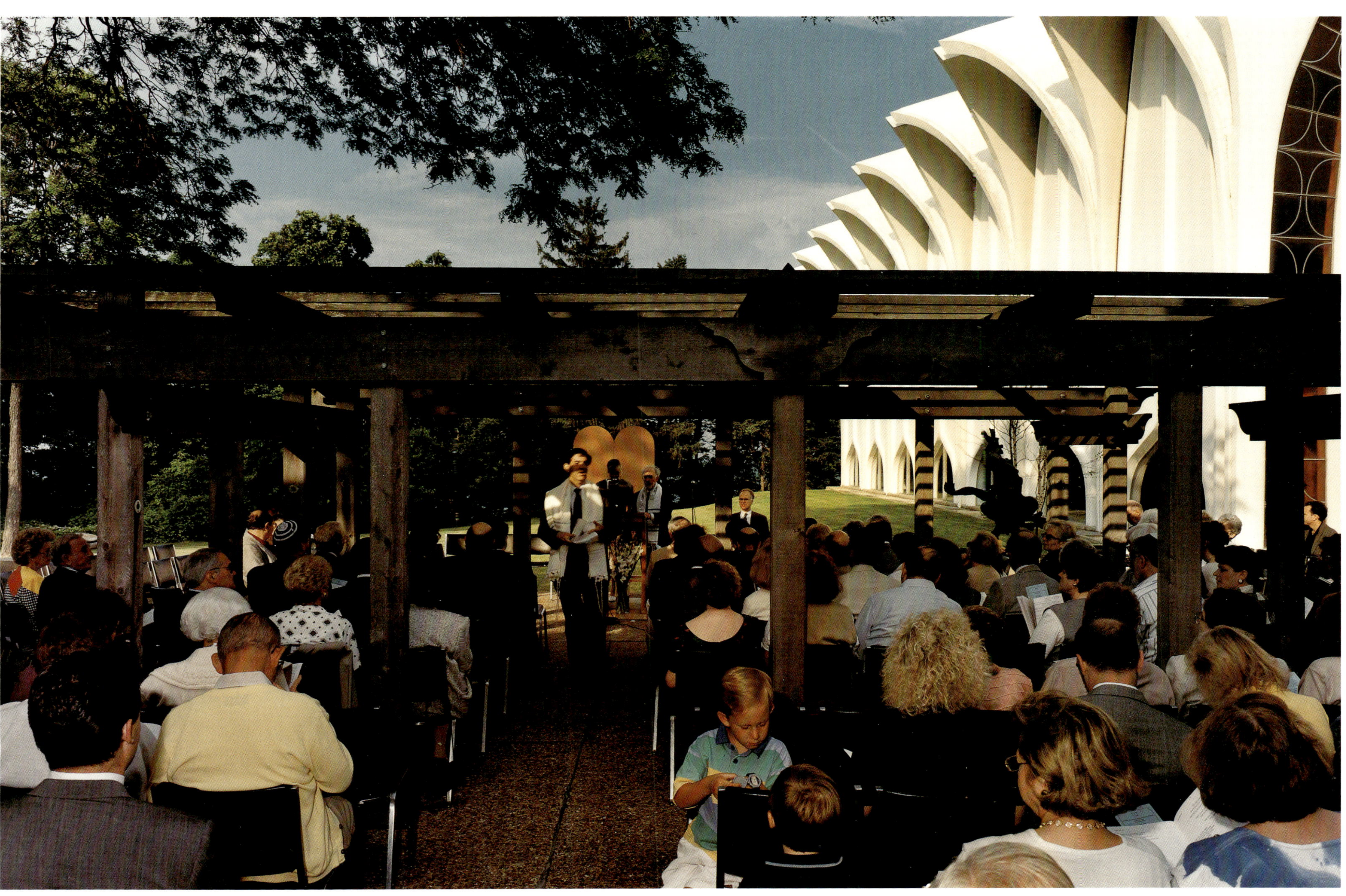

12 *Friday Evening Sabbath Service, North Shore Congregation Israel,* Glencoe, Illinois, 1995

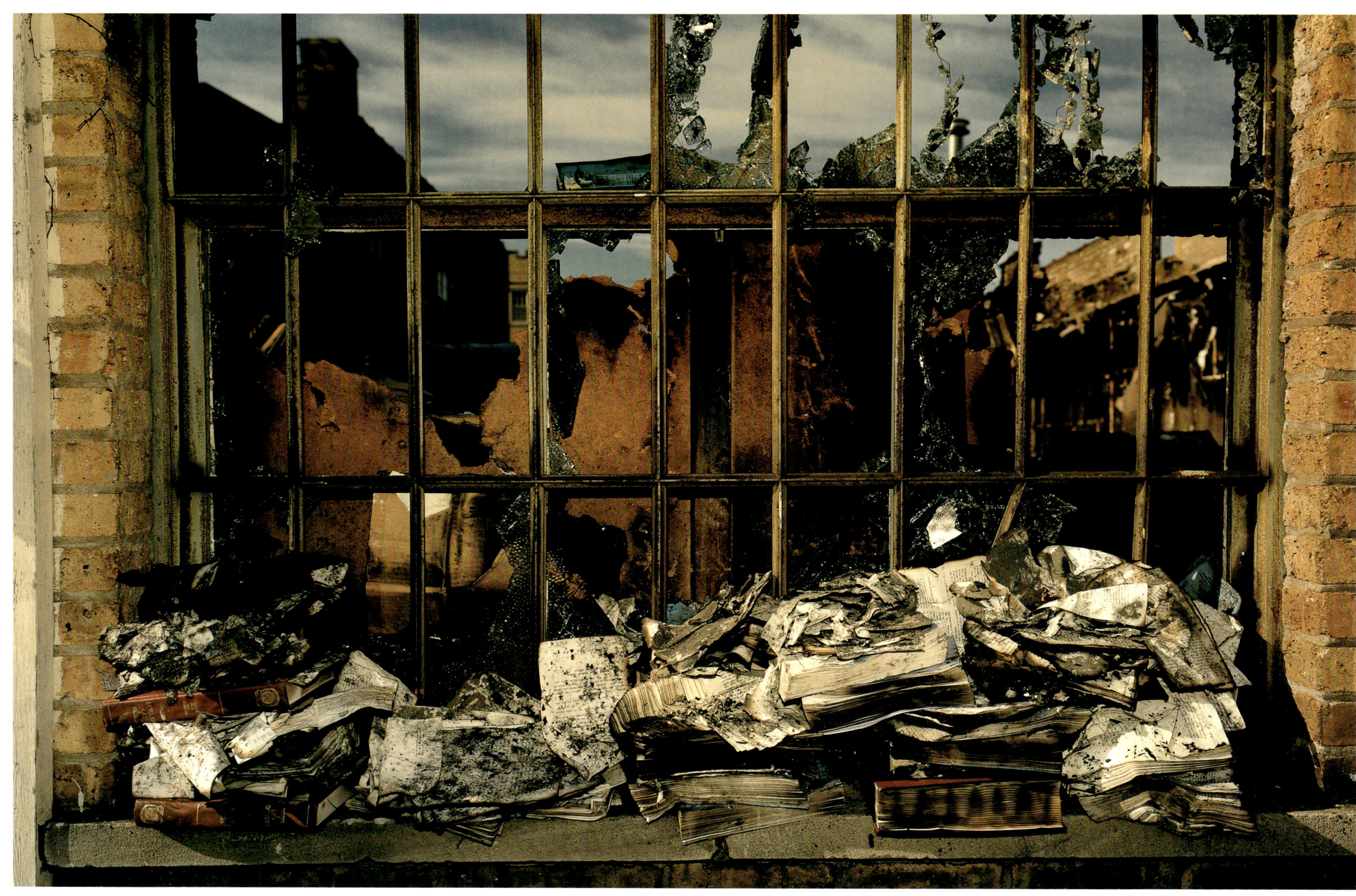

13 *Burnt Prayer Books, Post-Arson Fire, F.R.E.E. (Friends of Refugees of Eastern Europe) Congregation,* Chicago, 1993

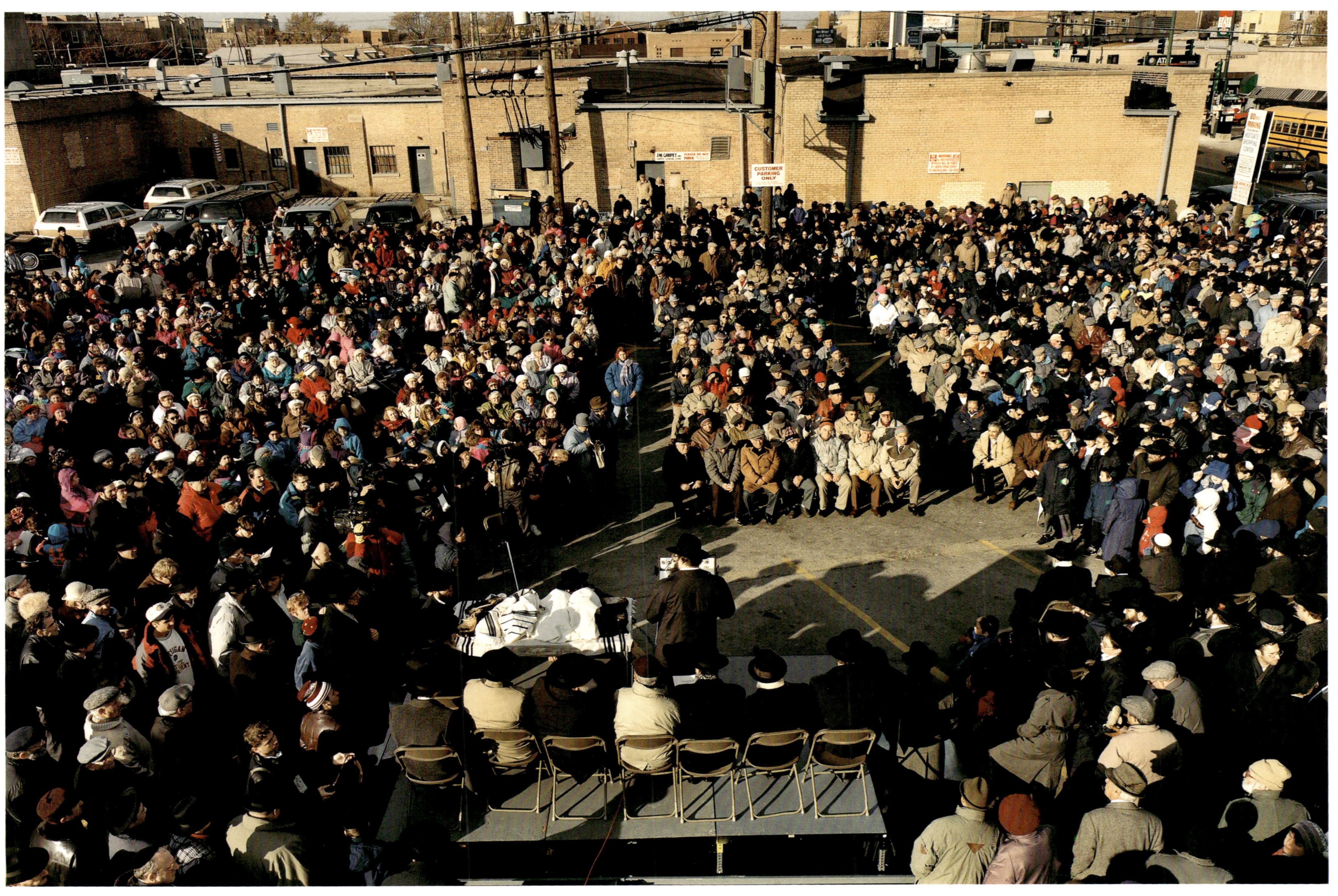

14 *Public Rally, Post-Arson Fire, F.R.E.E. (Friends of Refugees of Eastern Europe) Congregation,* Chicago, 1993

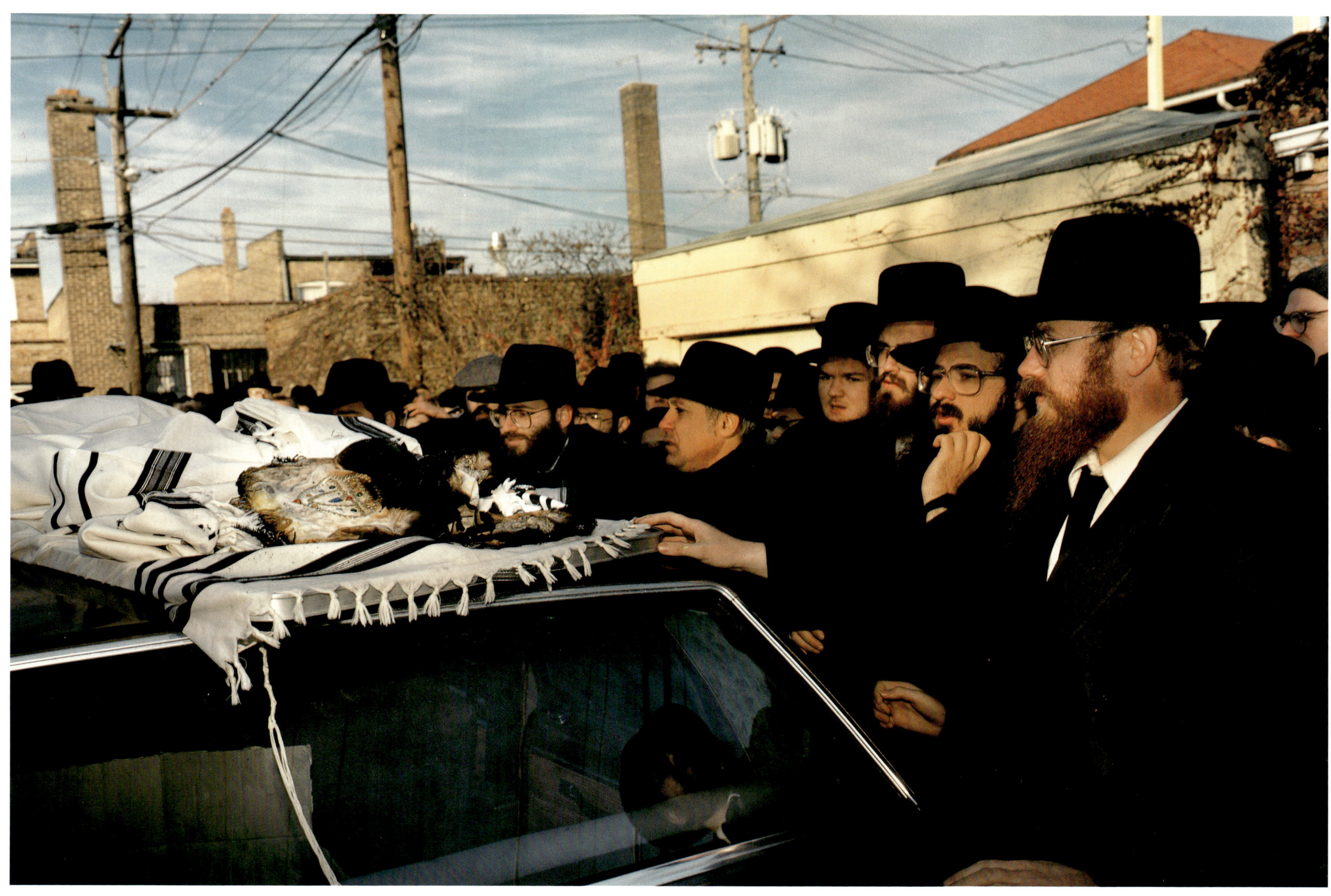

15 *Mourning Burnt Torahs, Post-Arson Fire, F.R.E.E. (Friends of Refugees of Eastern Europe) Congregation,* Chicago, 1993

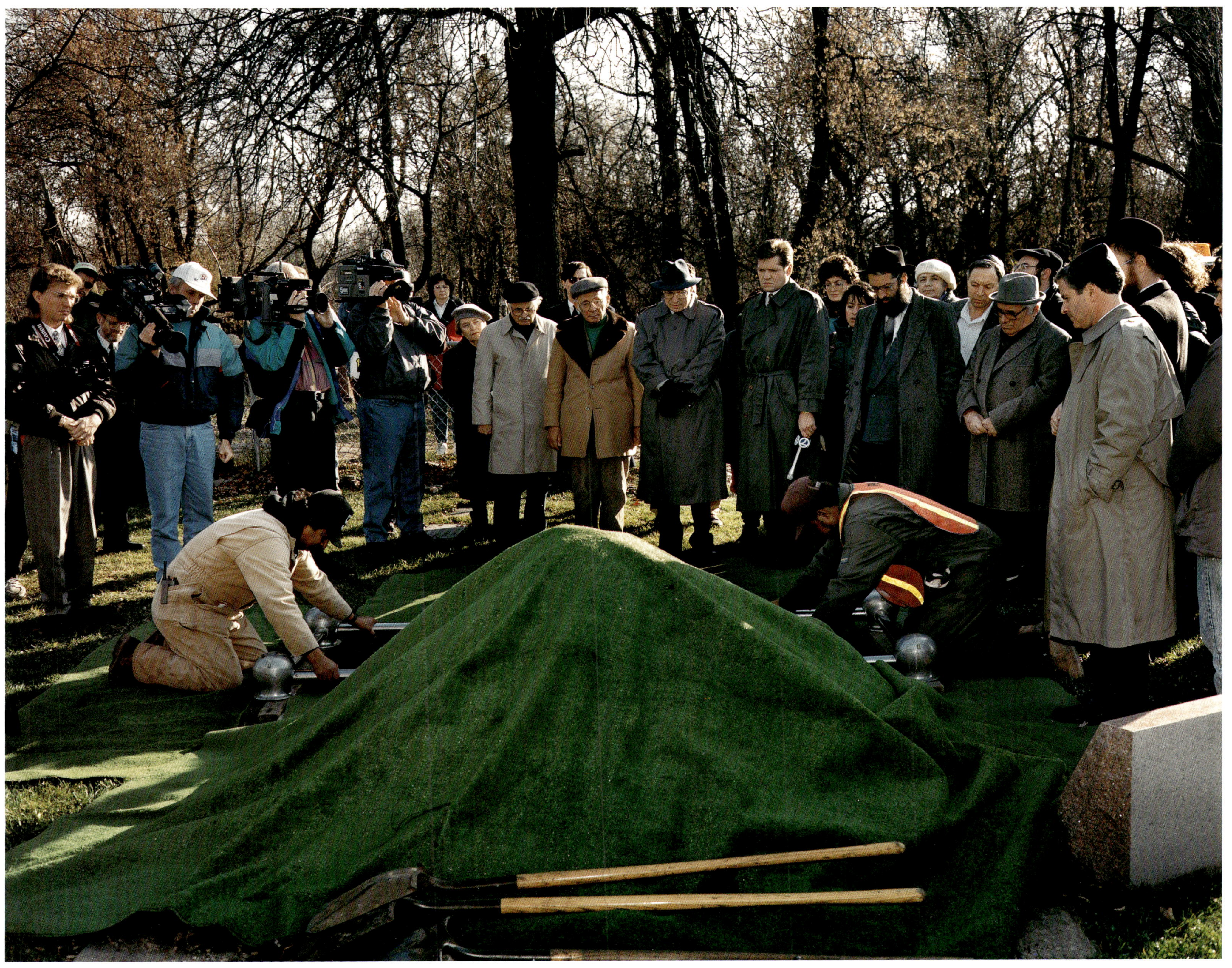

16 *Burial, Burnt Torahs, Post-Arson Fire, F.R.E.E. (Friends of Refugees of Eastern Europe) Congregation, Waldheim Cemetery,* Forest Park, Illinois, 1993

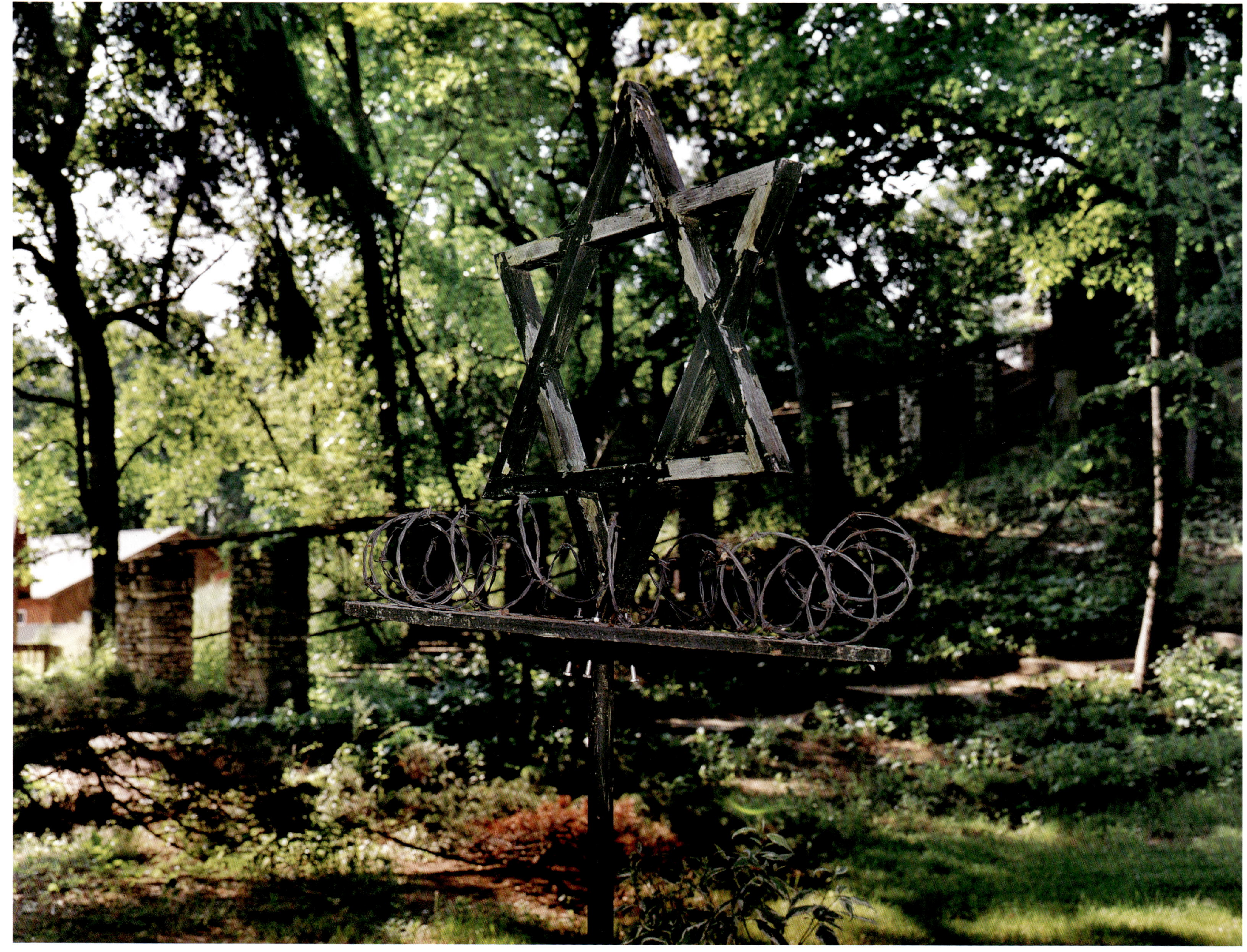

17 *Barbed-Wire Star, Camp Beber,* Mukwonago, Wisconsin, 1997

18 *Running Away, Yellow Star Stencil,* Chicago, 1994

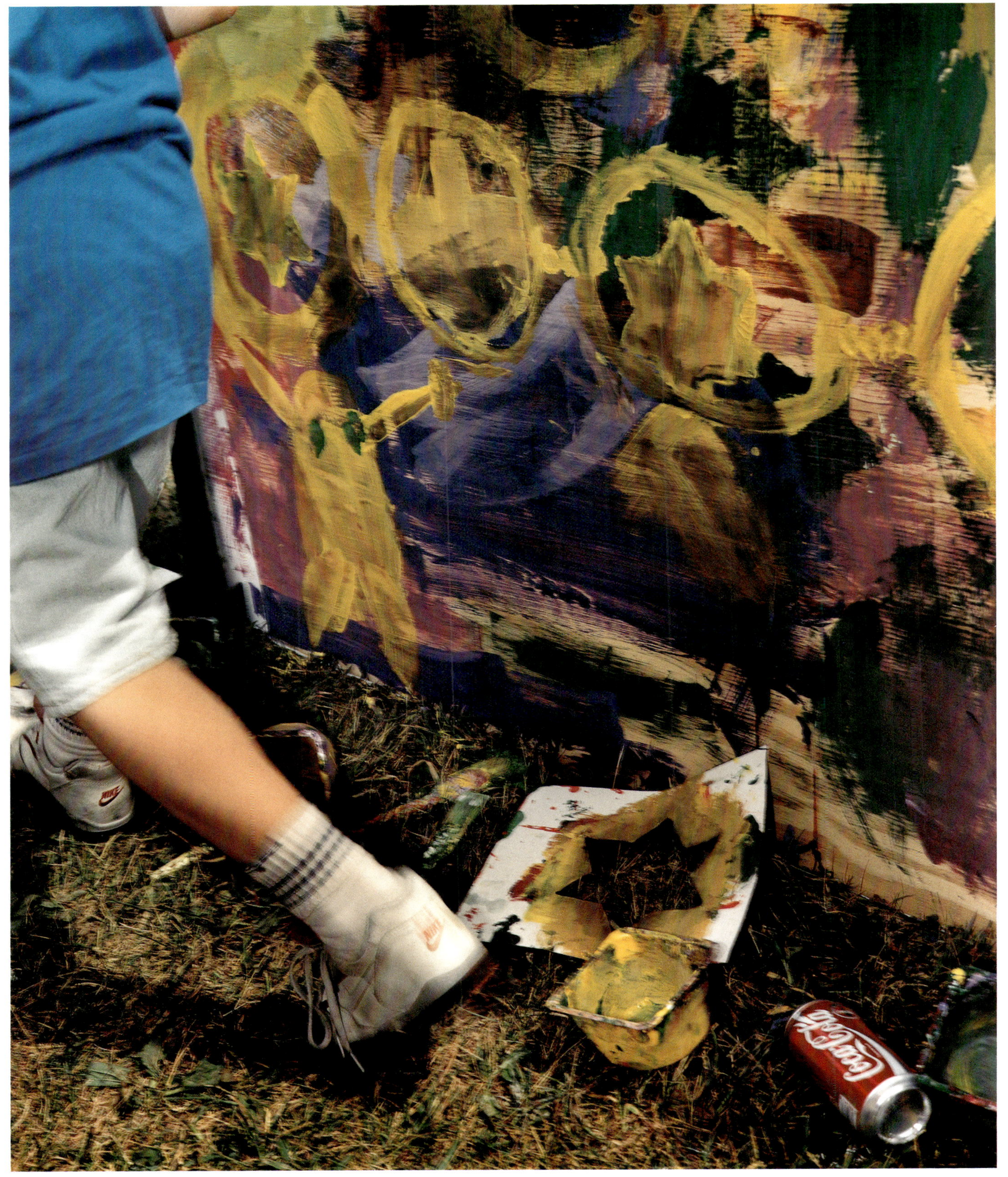
NIKE
Coca-Cola

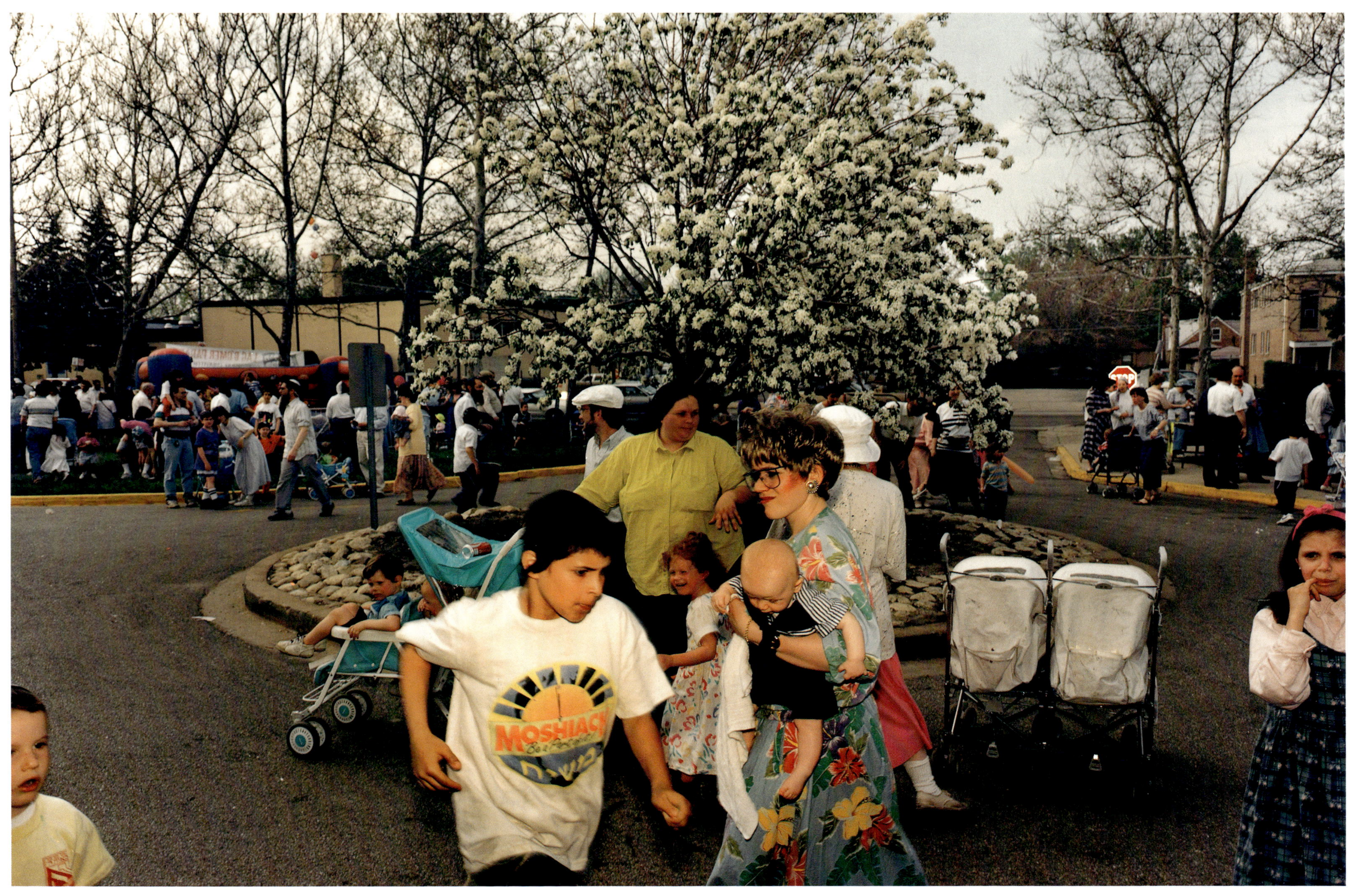

19 *Lag B'Omer Festival, Horwich J.C.C.,* Chicago, 1993

20 *Sukkah, Chicago Loop Synagogue,* 1994

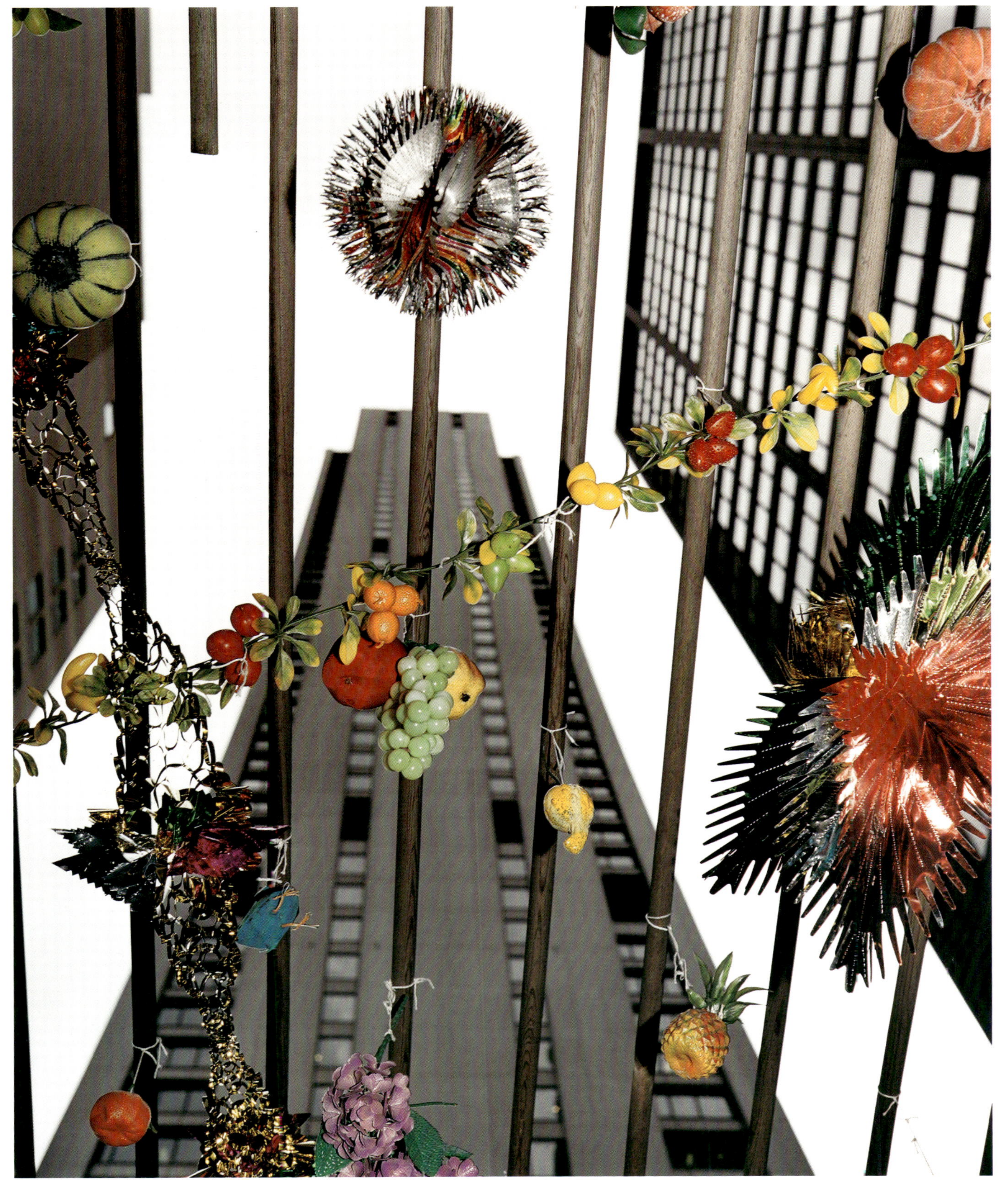

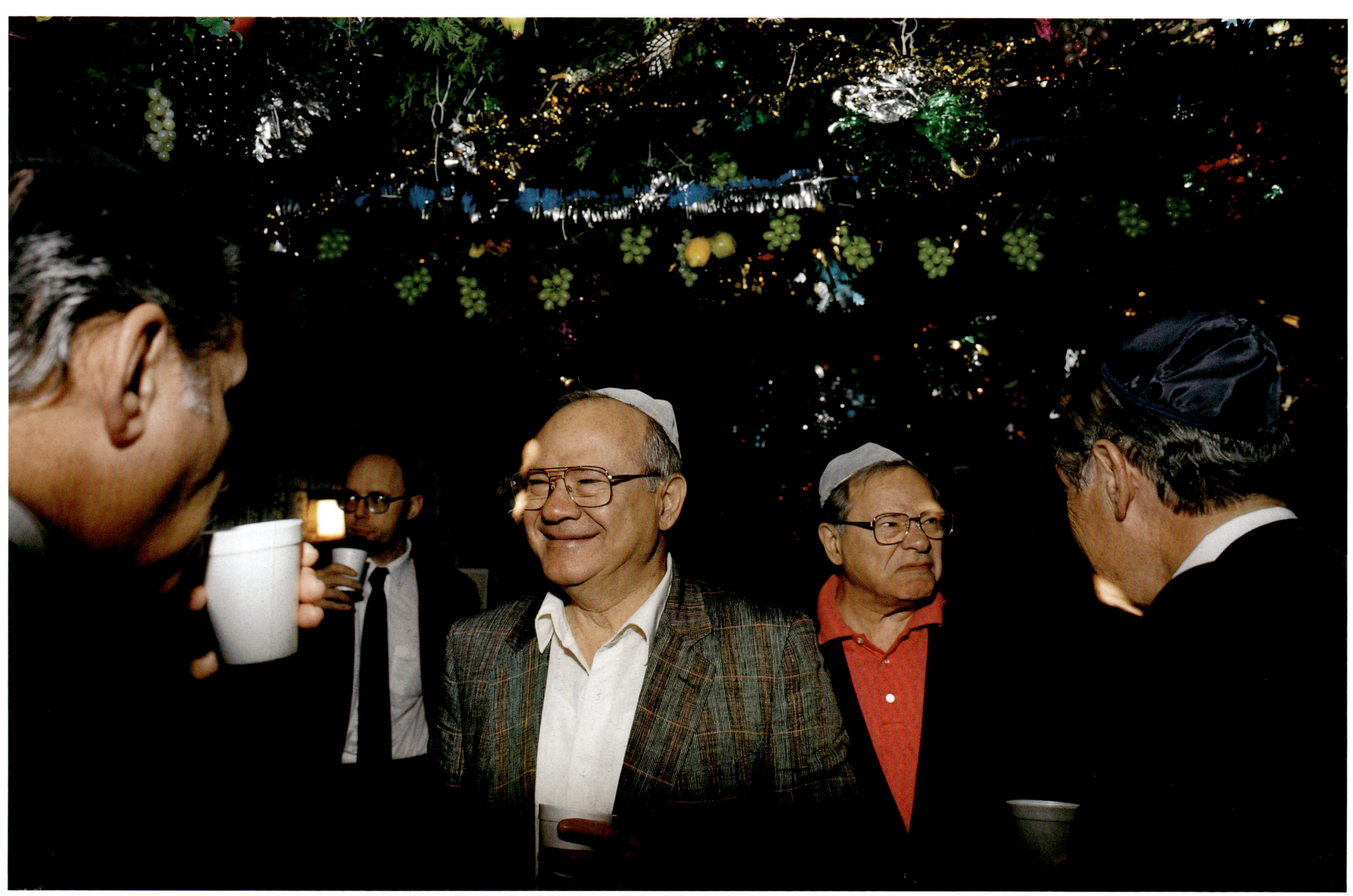

21 *Men in the Sukkah, Chicago Loop Synagogue,* 1995

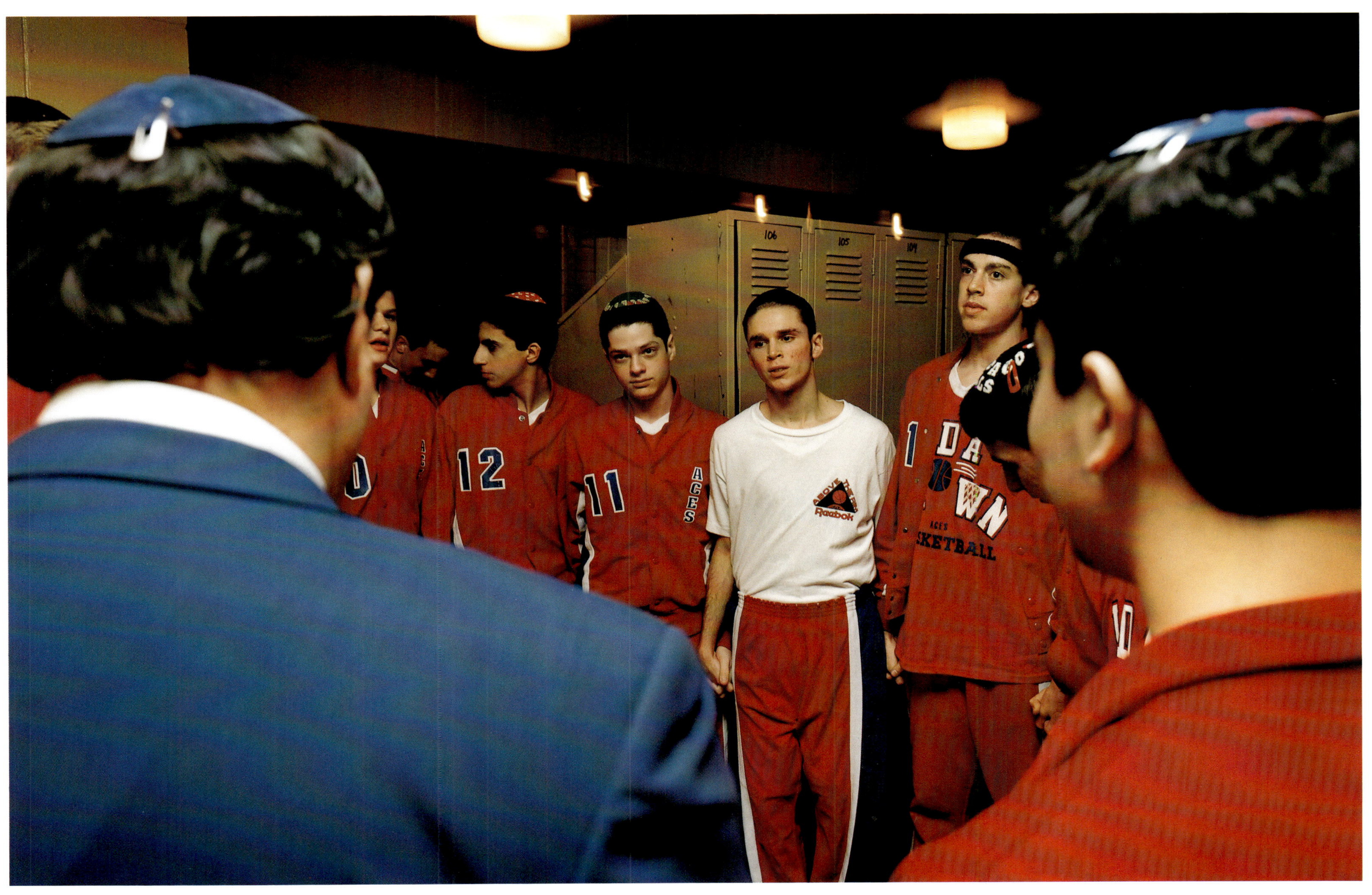

22 *Half-Time Prayer, Regional High School Basketball Finals,* Chicago, 1996

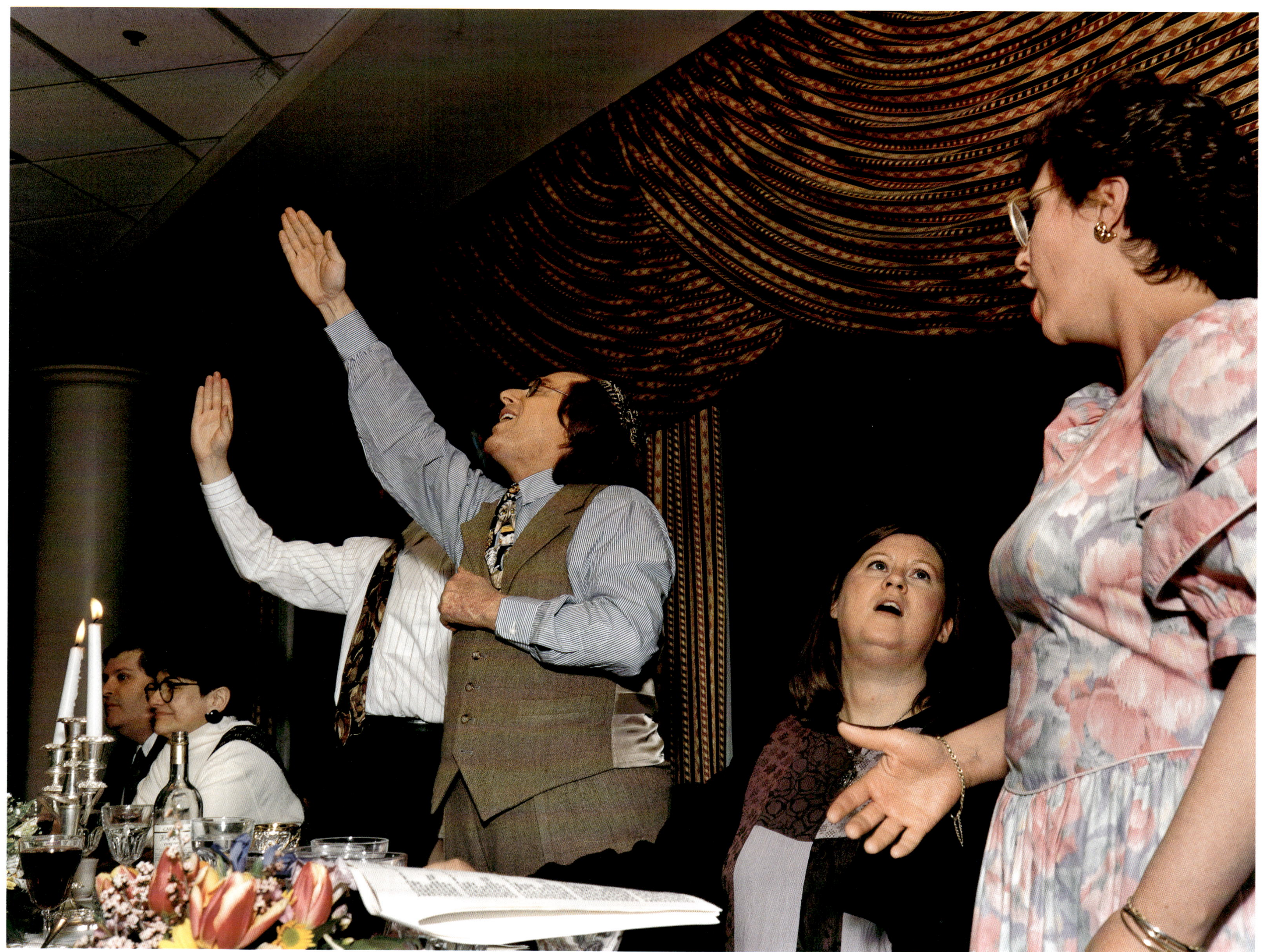

23 *Passover Seder in American Sign Language, Congregation B'Nai Shalom,* Chicago, 1995

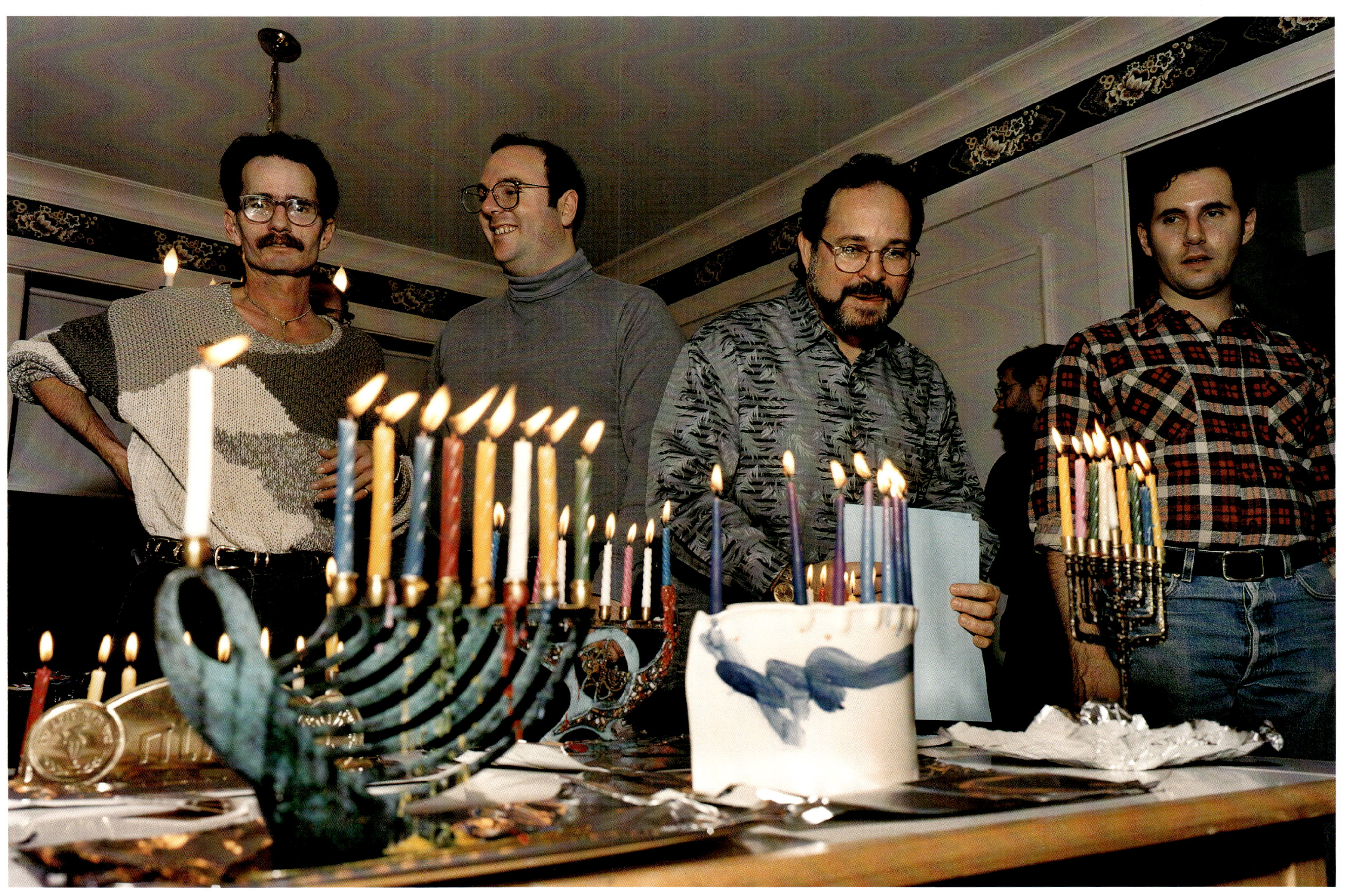

24 *Chanukah Candle Lighting, Congregation Or Chadash,* Chicago, 1995

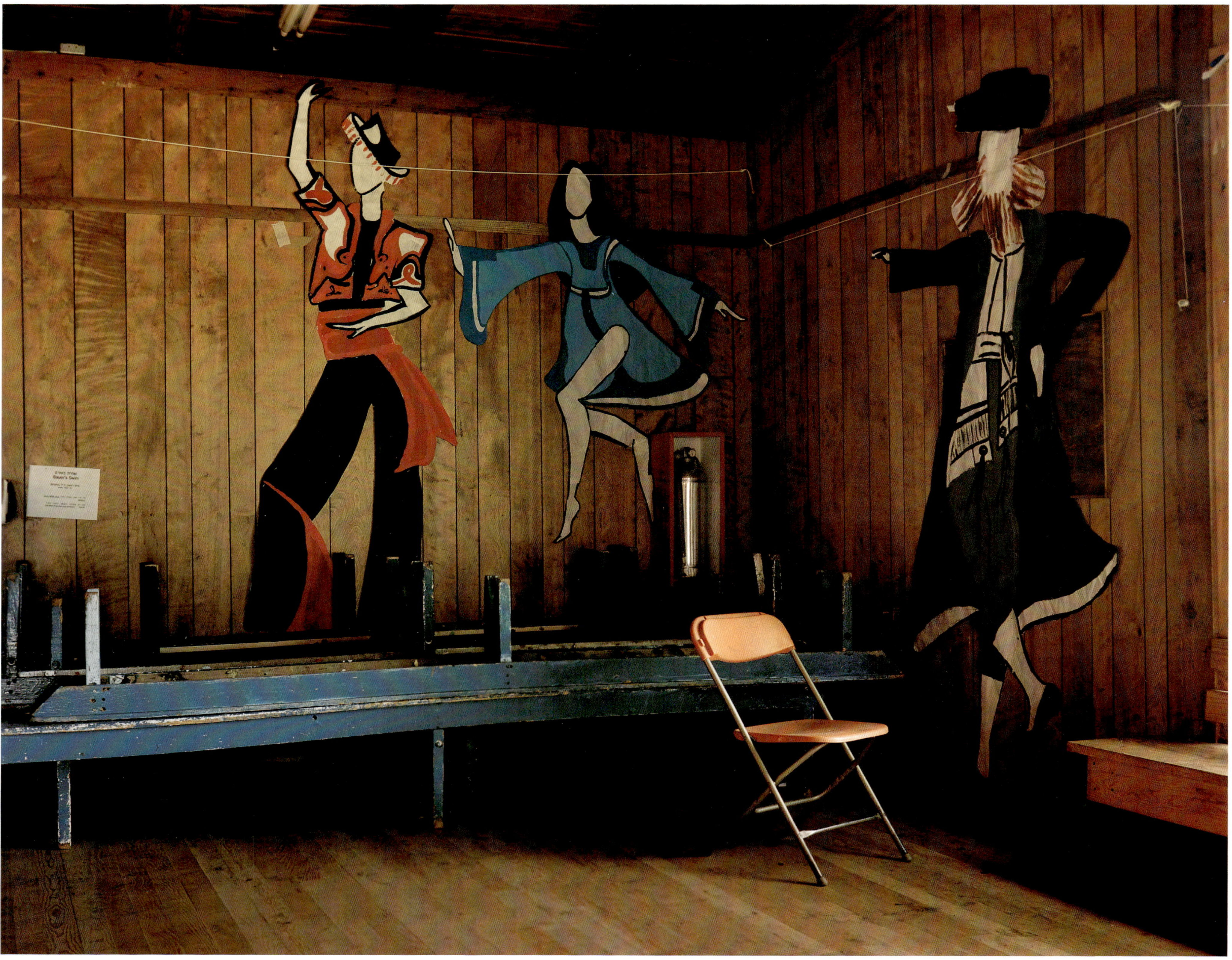
Bauer's Swim

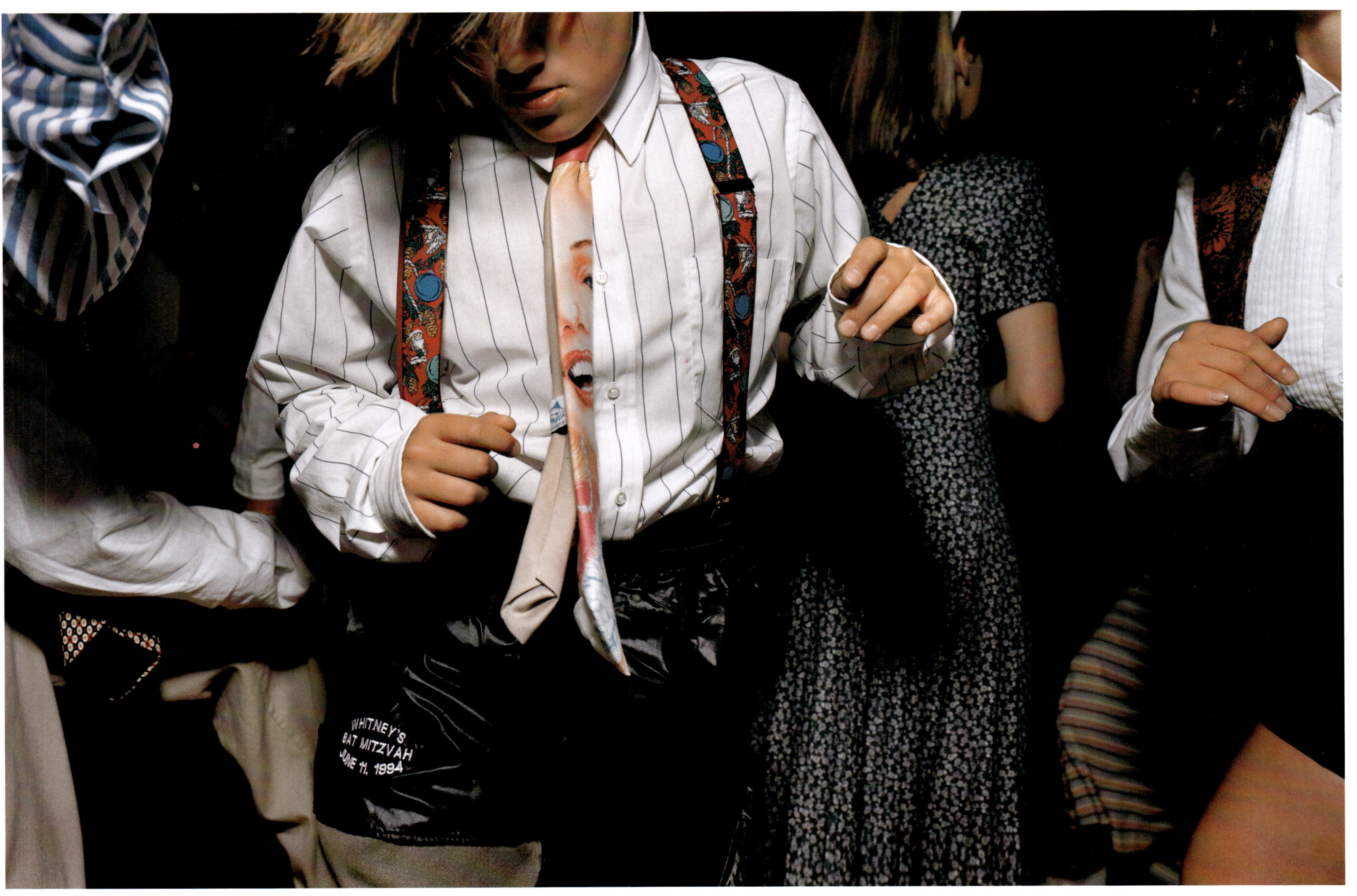

25 *Recreation Hall, Camp Ramah,* Rhinelander, Wisconsin, 1994

26 *Boxers, Whitney's Bat Mitzvah,* Kenilworth, Illinois, 1994

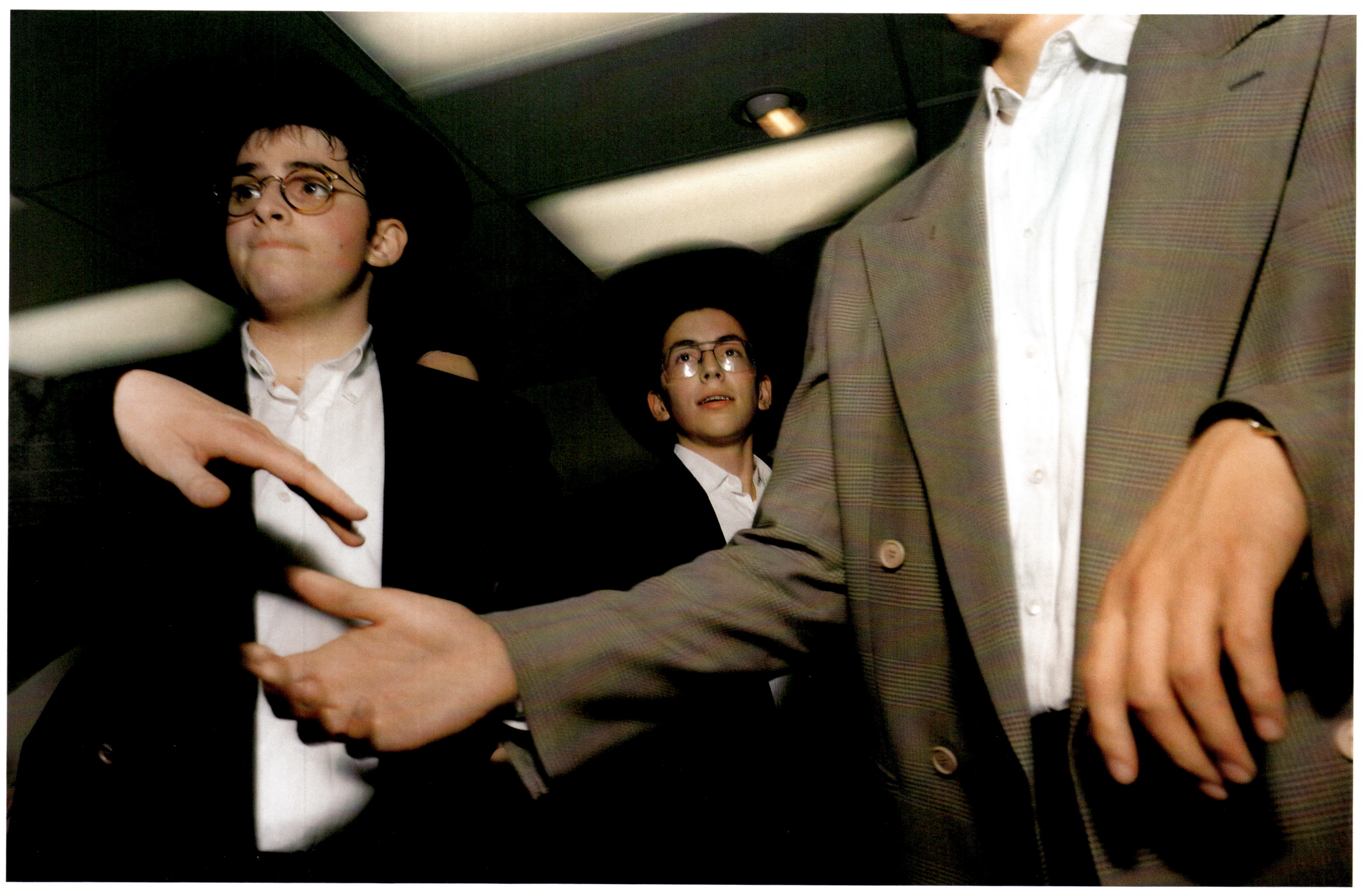

27 *Boys Dancing, Sukkoth Celebration, Yeshiva Migdal Torah,* Chicago, 1993

28 *Performing for the Bride and Groom, Spirn Wedding,* Chicago, 1997

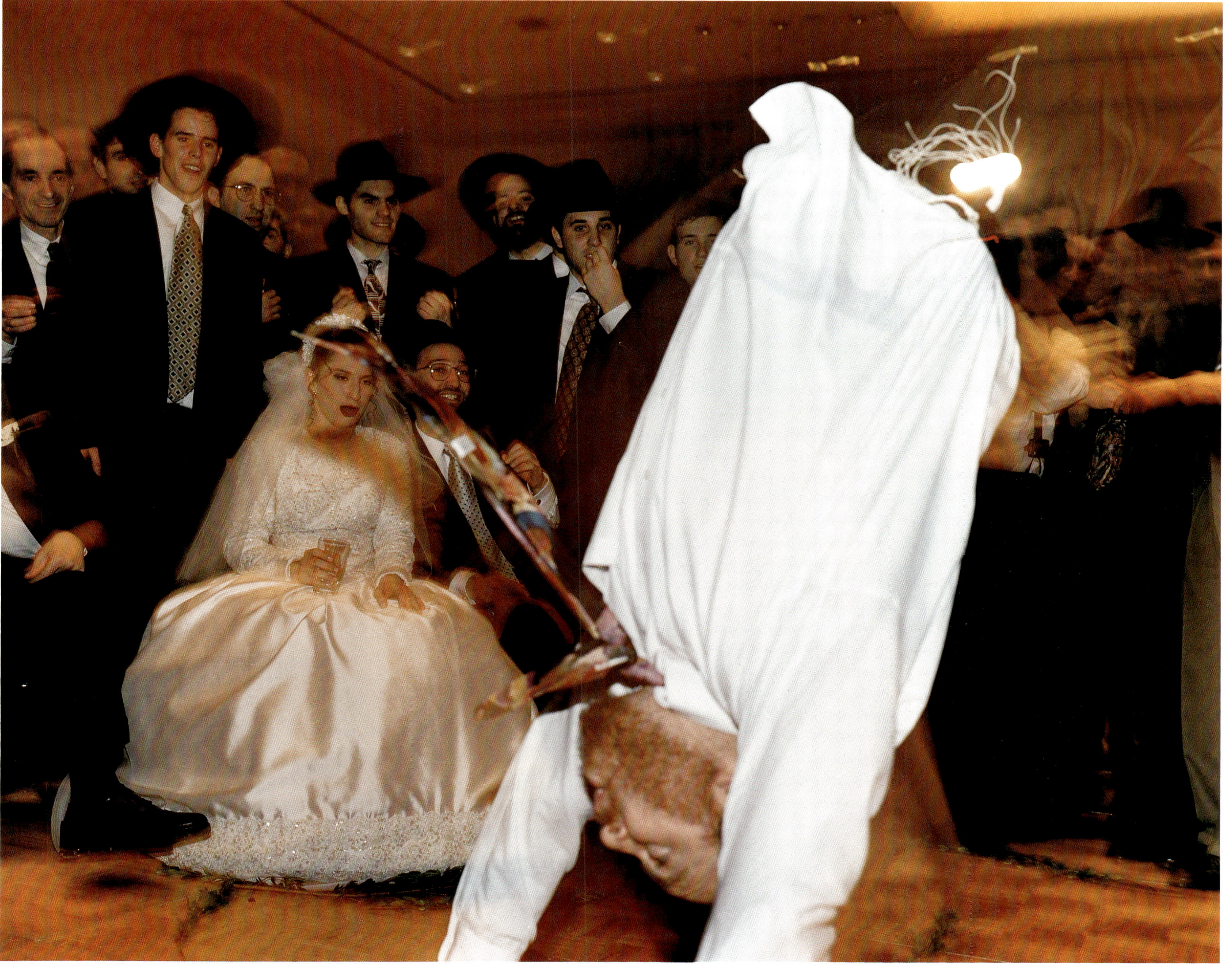

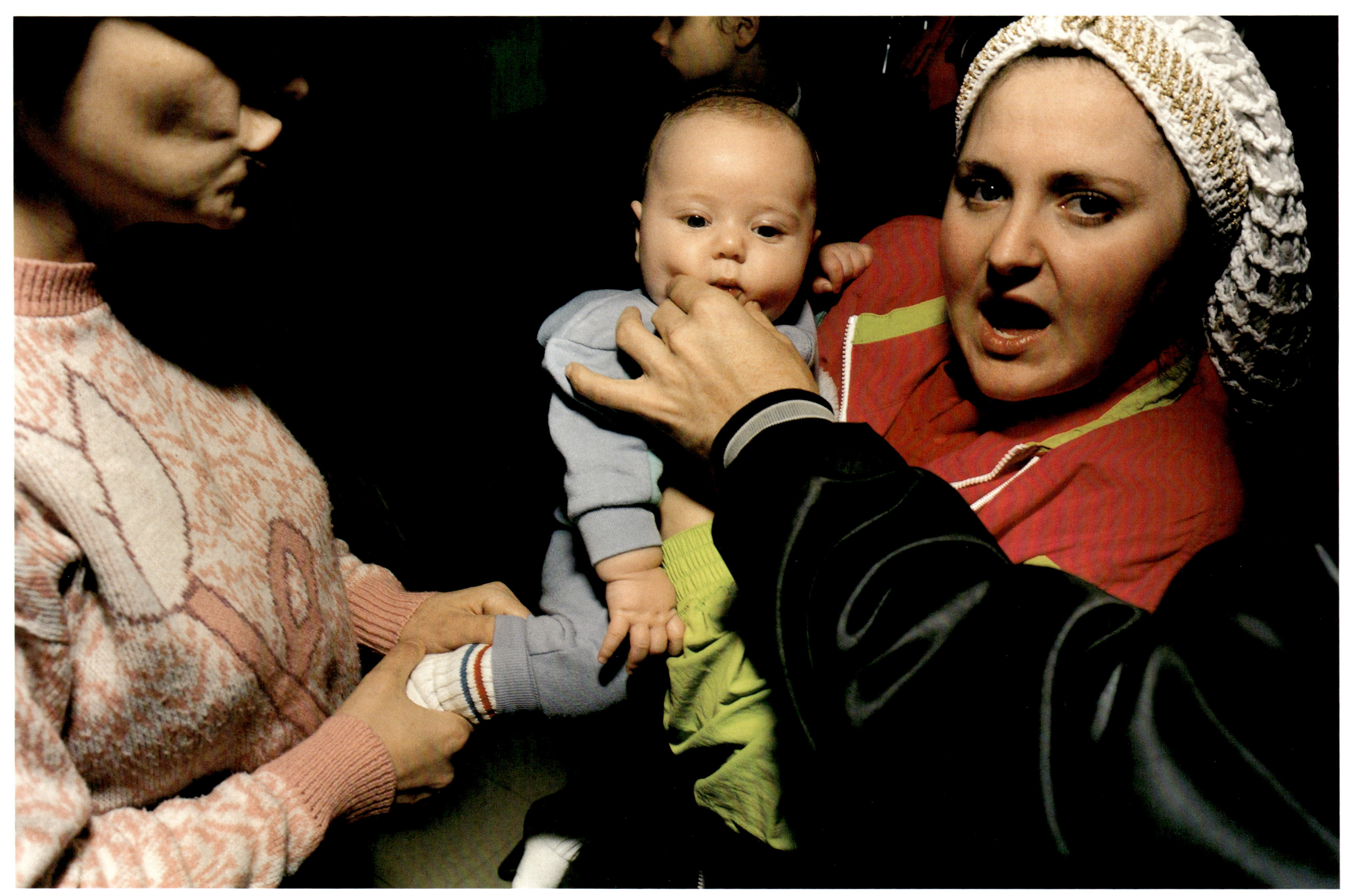

29 *Mouths, Sukkoth Celebration, Migdal Torah,* Chicago, 1993

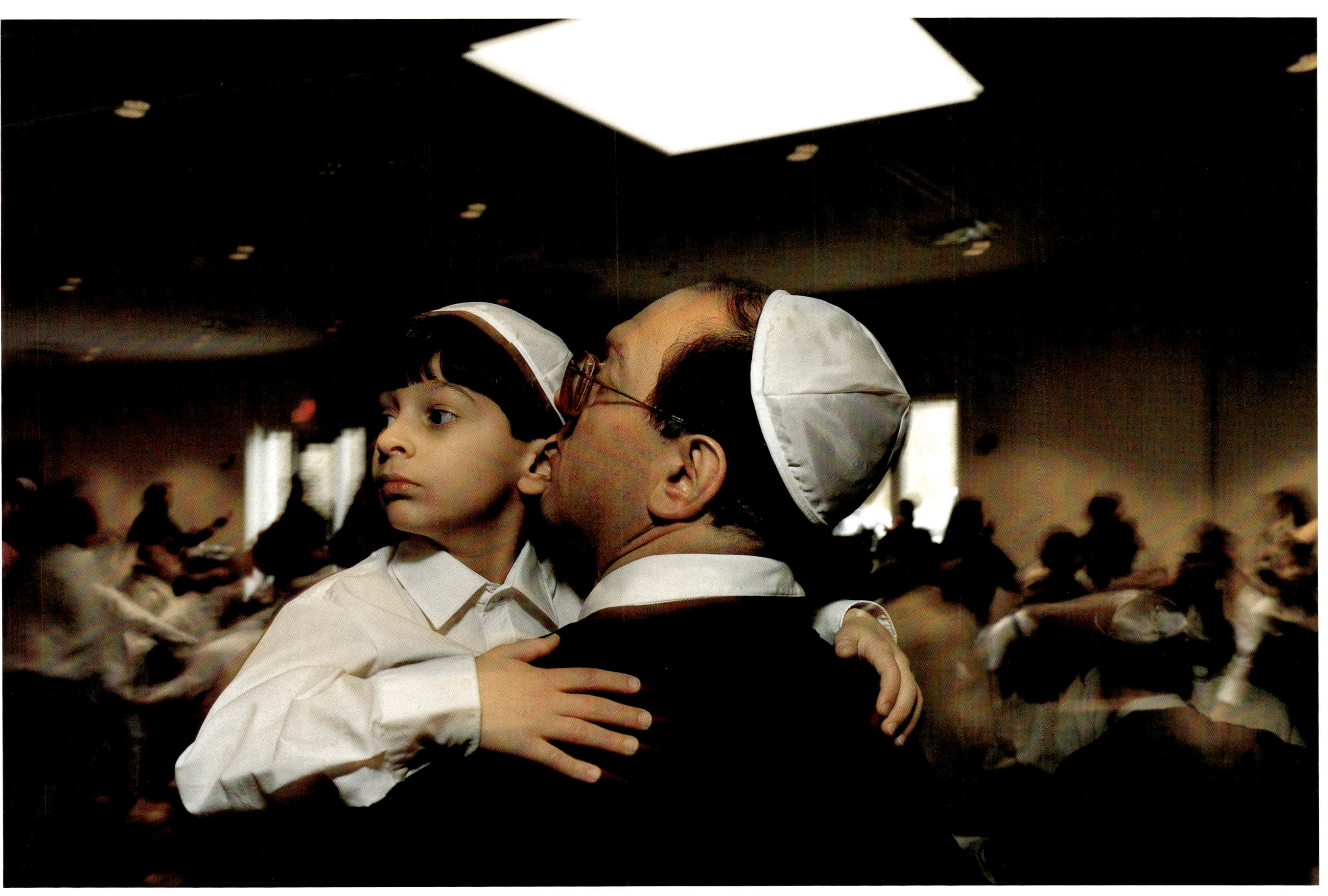

30 *Father and Son, Chanukah Celebration, Congregation B'Nai Tikvah,* Deerfield, Illinois, 1995

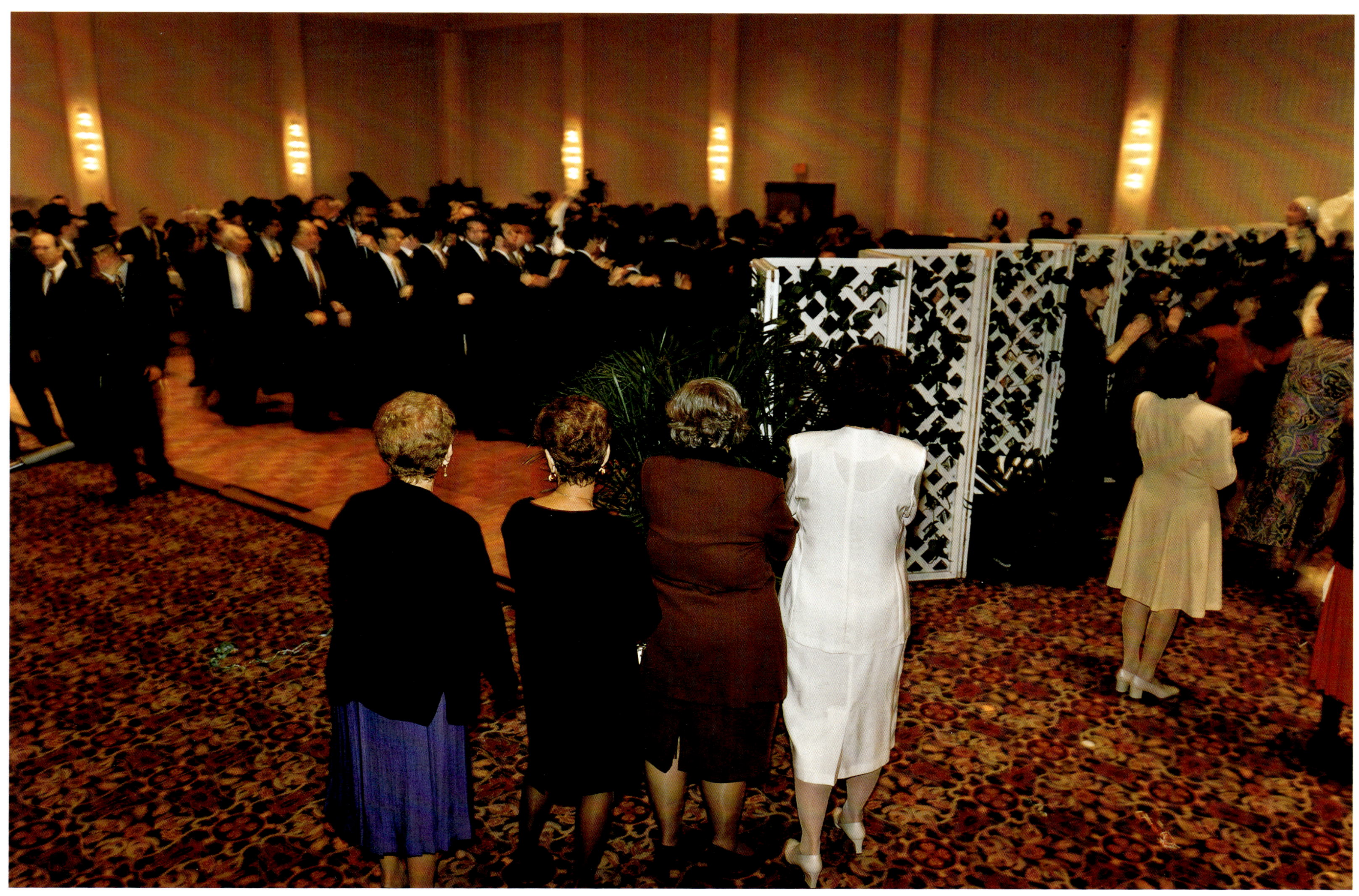

31 *Women Watching, Men Dancing, Spirn Wedding,* Rosemont, Illinois, 1997

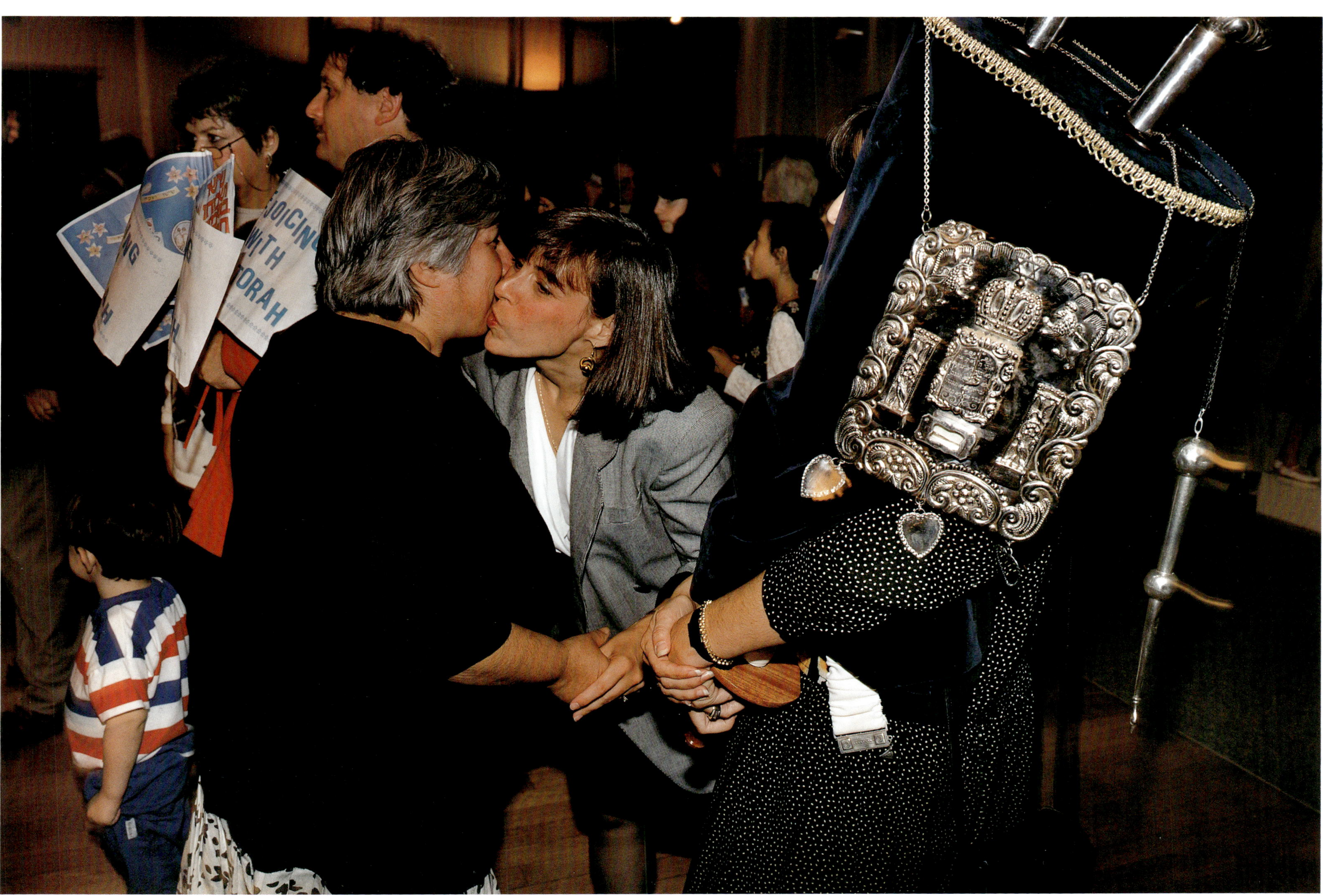

32 *Simhat Torah, North Shore Congregation Israel,* Glencoe, Illinois, 1994

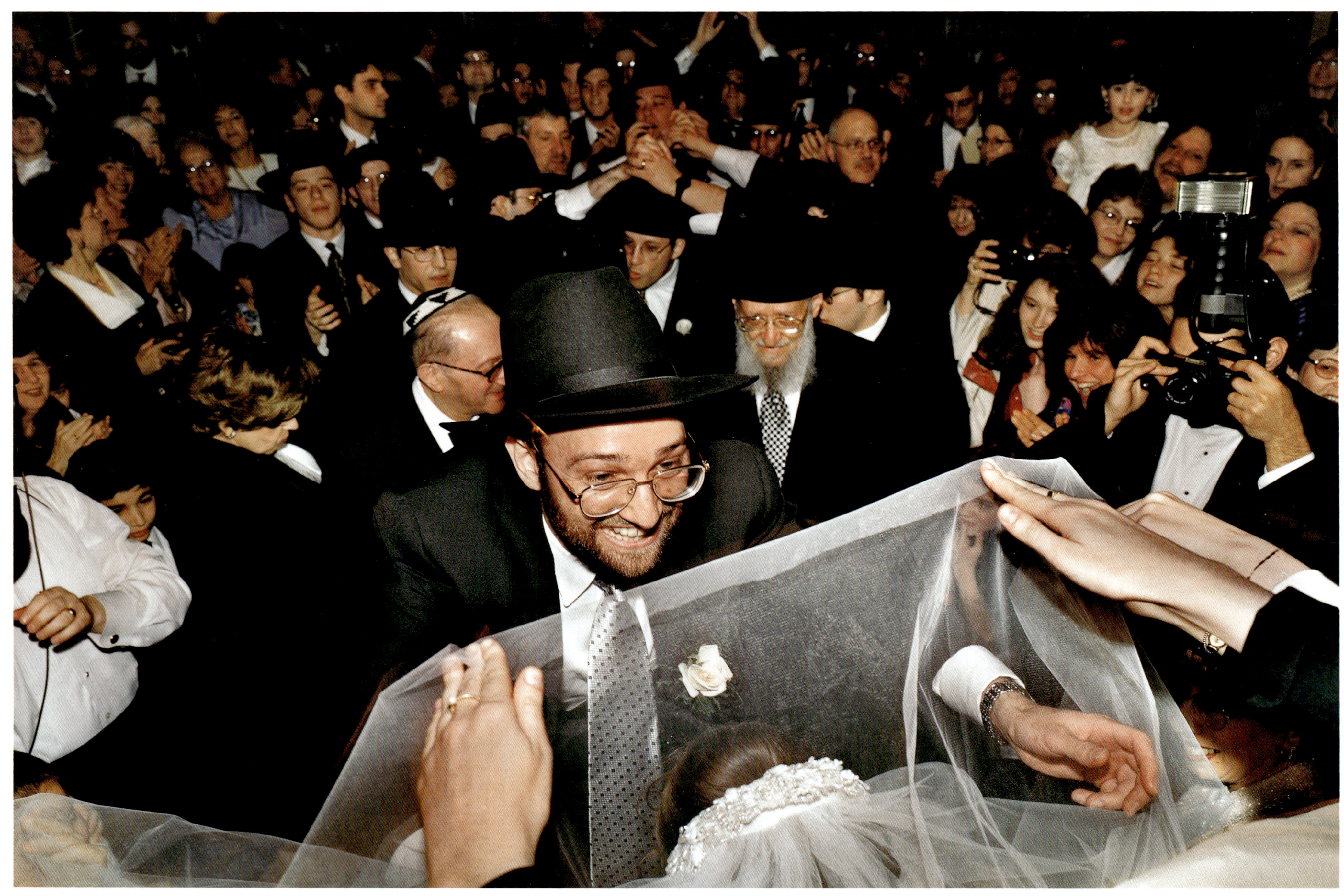

33 *Badeken (Veiling), Spirn Wedding,* Chicago, 1997

34 *Post-Yom Kippur Singles Dance,* Lincolnwood, Illinois, 1993

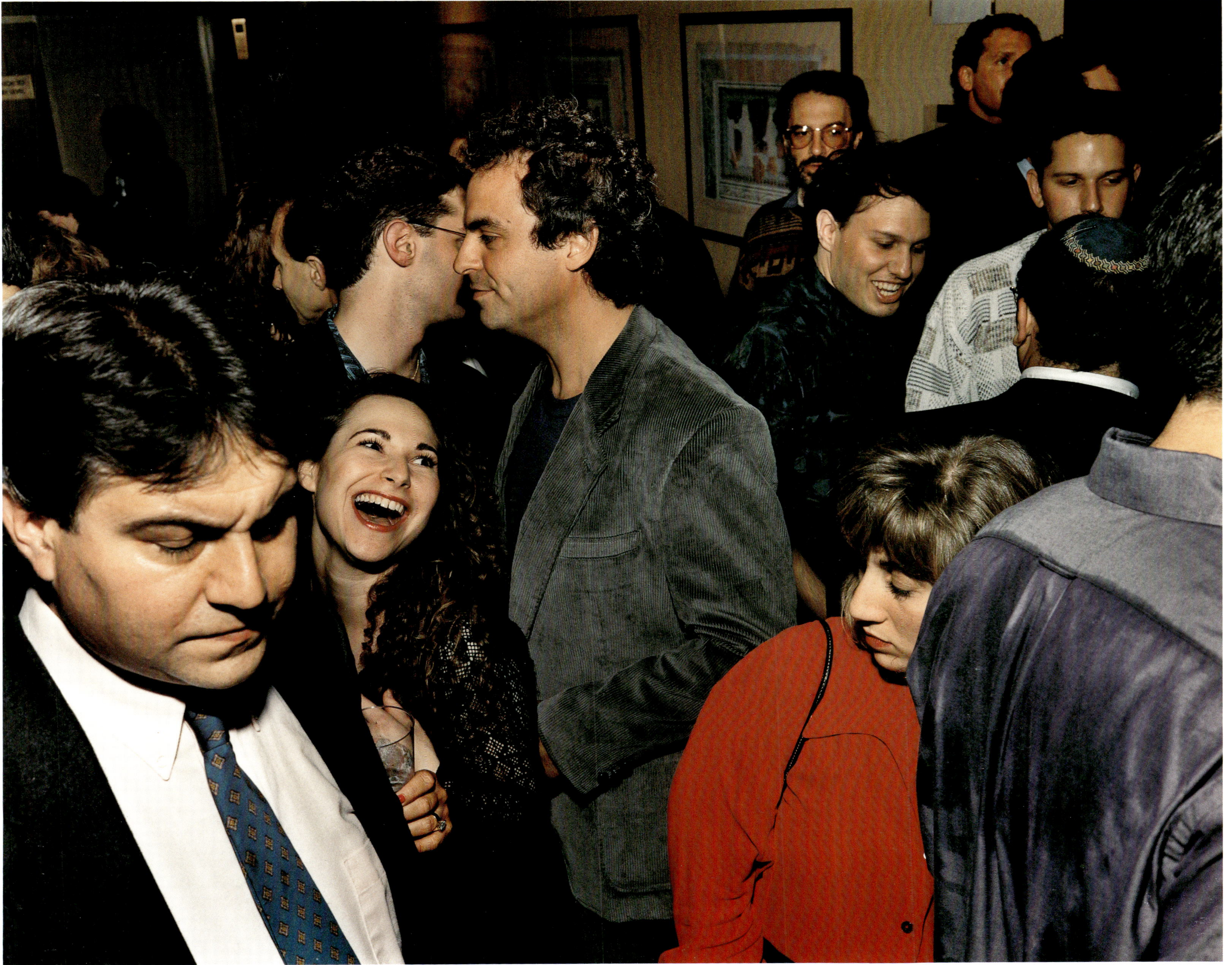

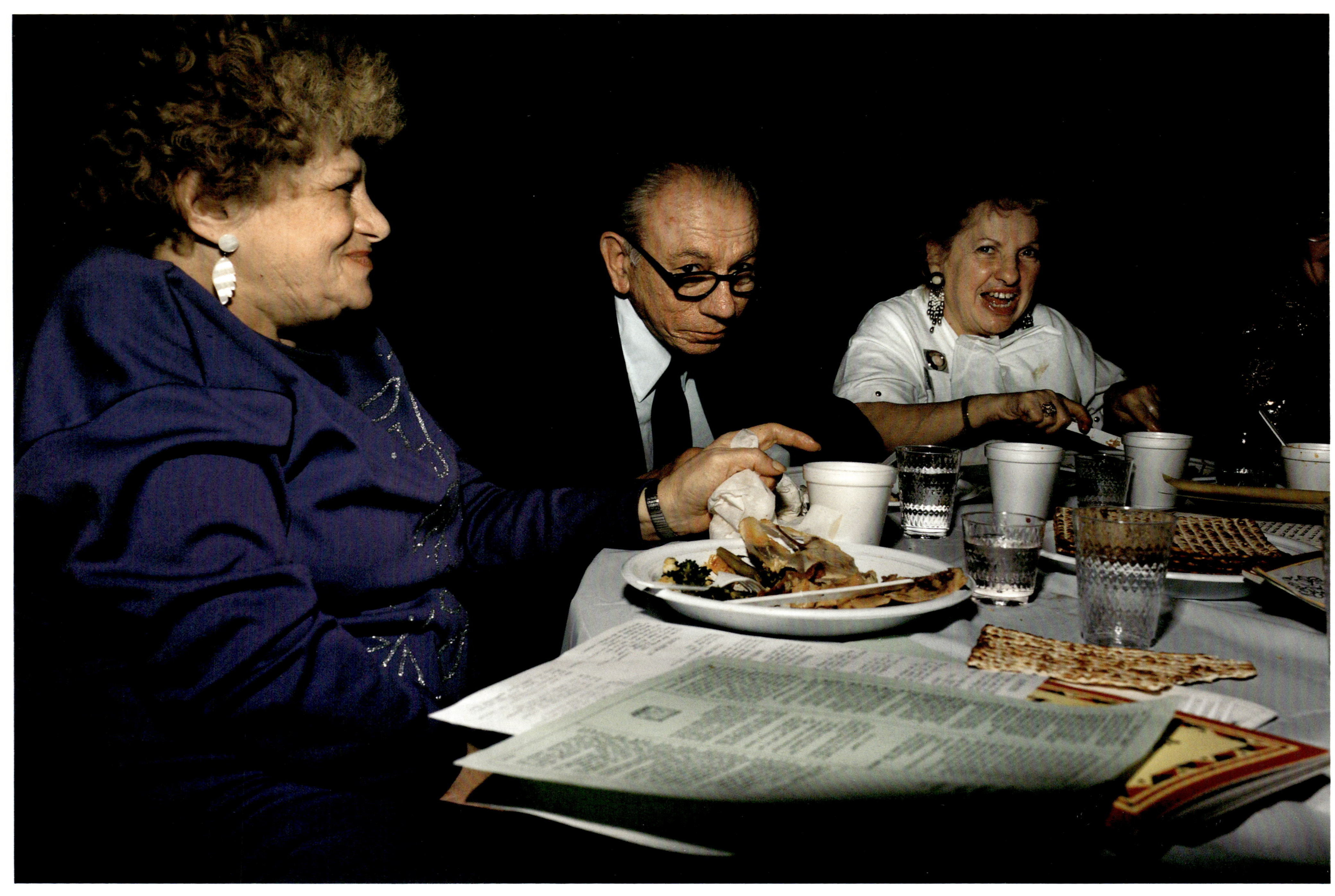

35 *Communal Seder, Man, Two Women,* Chicago, 1993

36 *Conversation, Whitney's Bat Mitzvah,* Kenilworth, Illinois, 1994

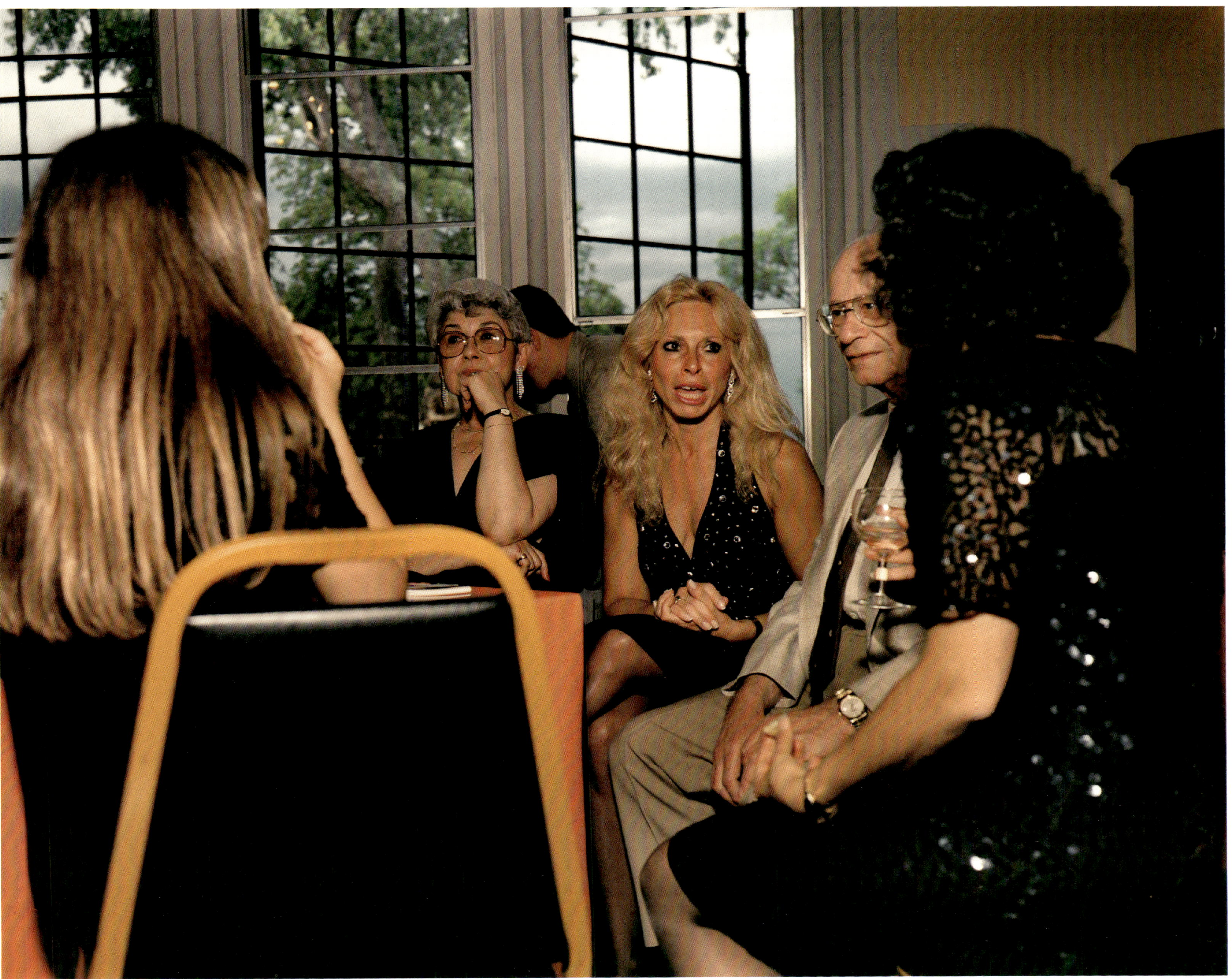

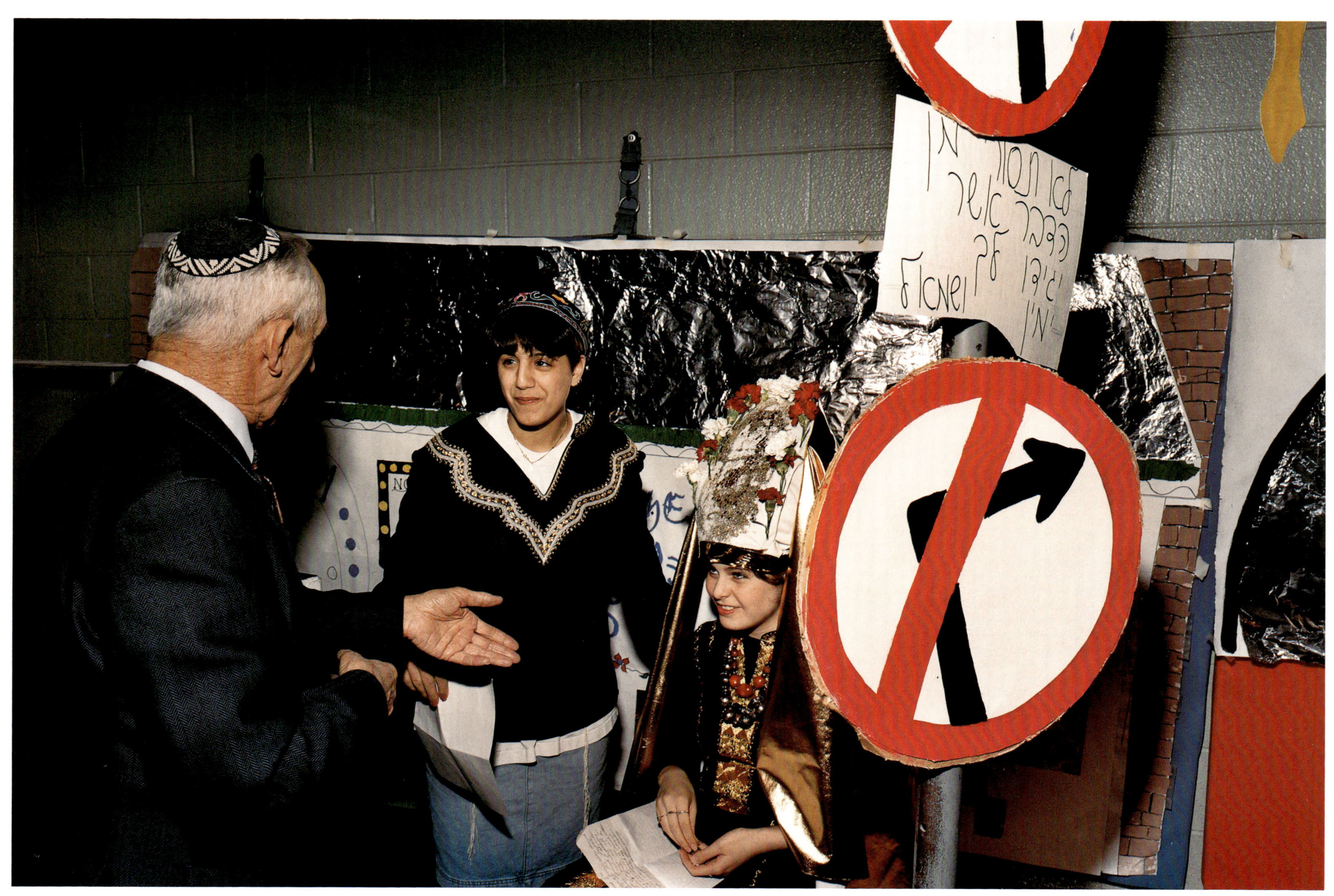

37 *Cultural Presentation, Ida Crown Academy,* Chicago, 1994

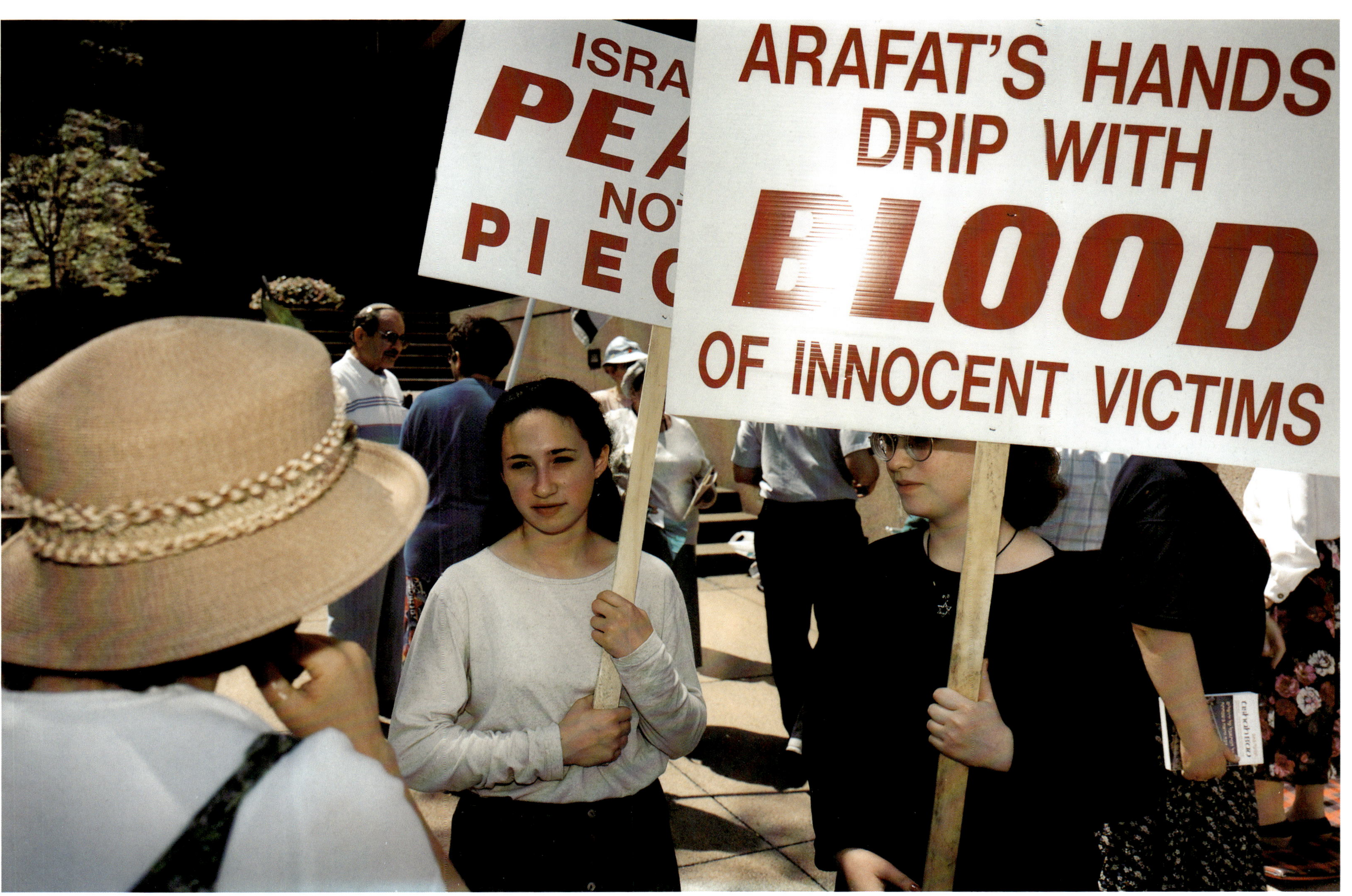

38 *Pro-Israel Demonstration, Tisha B'Av*, Chicago, 1995

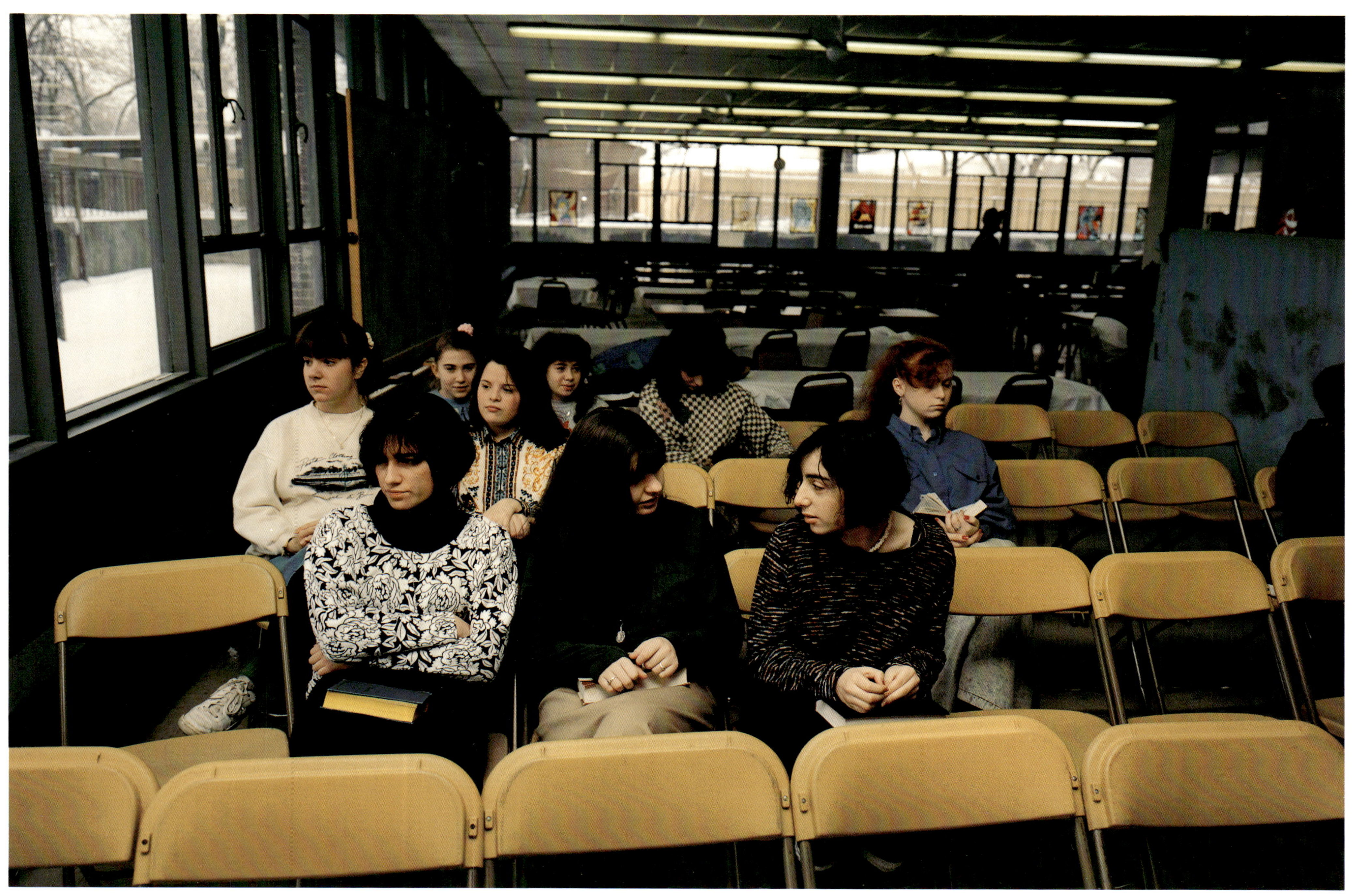

39 *Girls, Morning Service, Ida Crown Academy,* Chicago, 1994

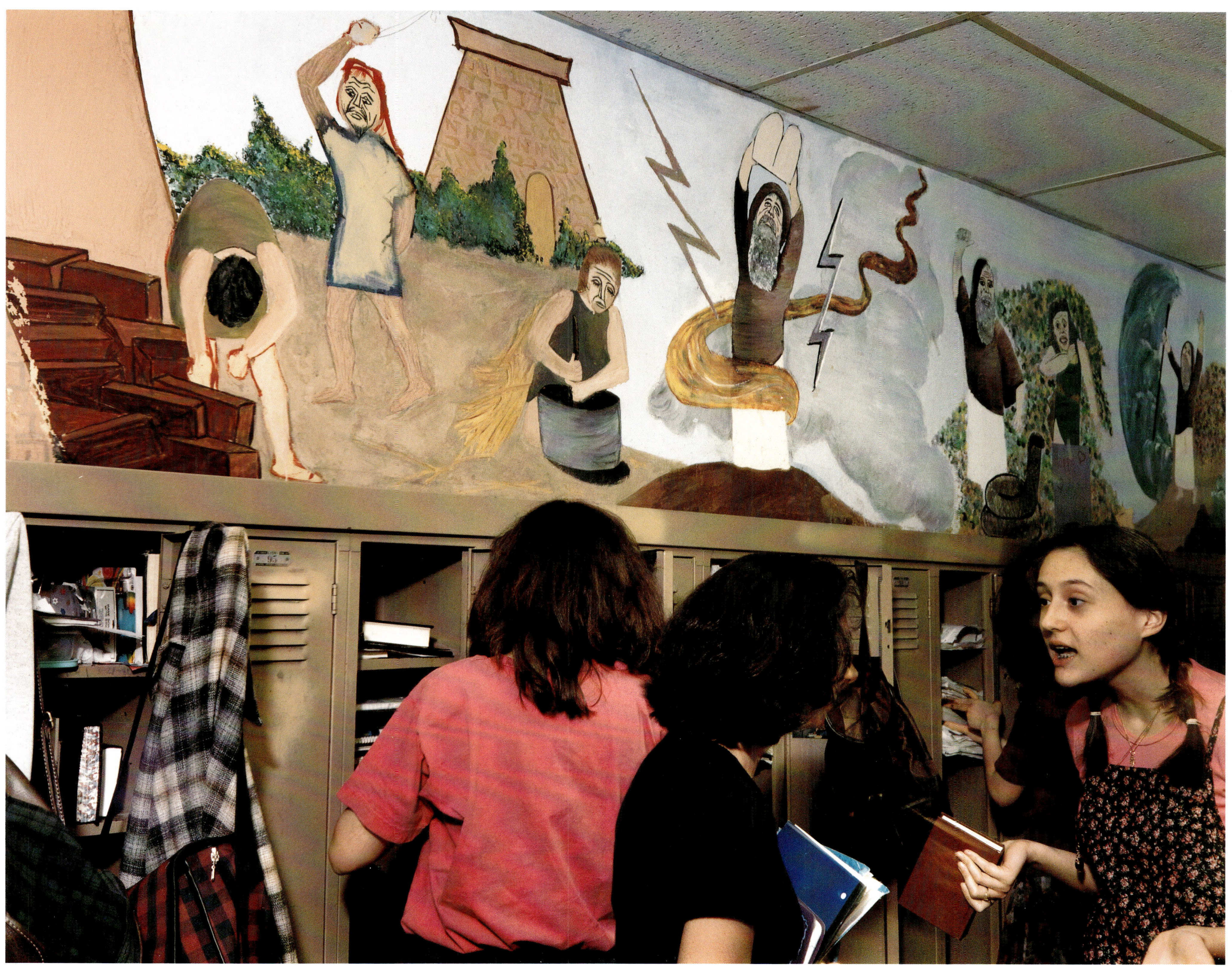

40 *Girls in Hallway, Ida Crown Academy,* Chicago, 1995

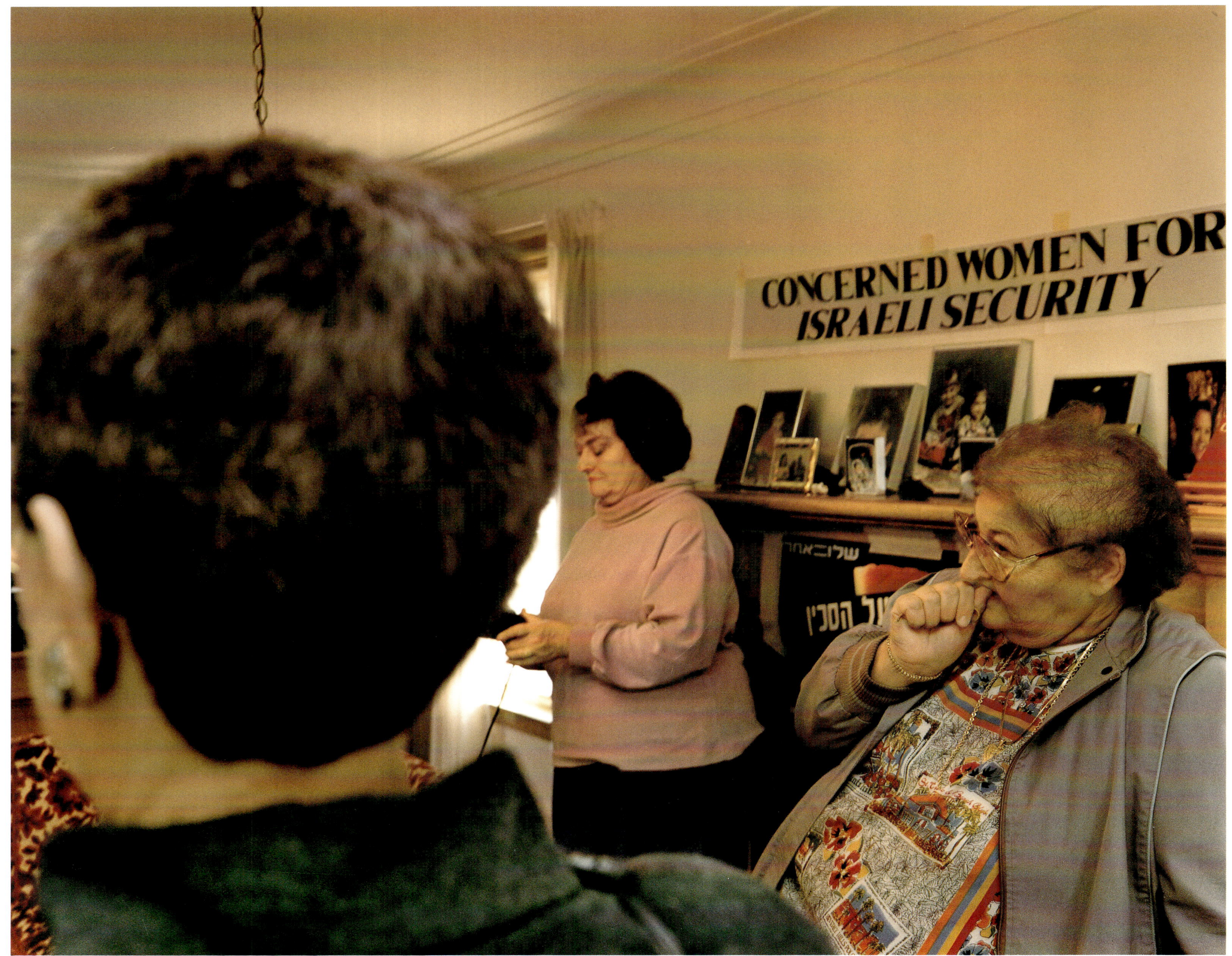

41 *Meeting, Concerned Women for Israeli Security,* Chicago, 1995

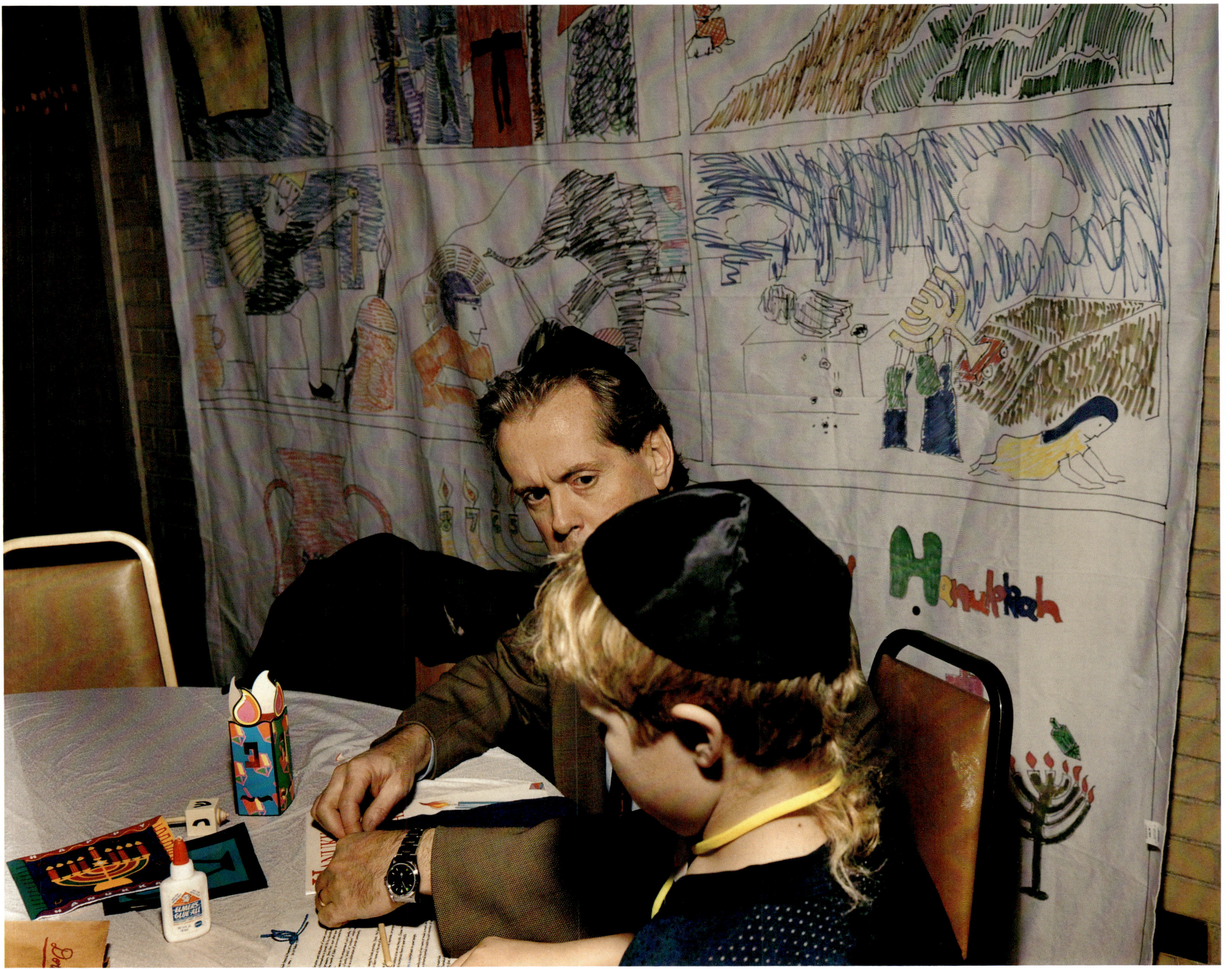

42 *Father and Son, Chanukah Preparation, Congregation Rodfei Zedek,* Chicago, 1994

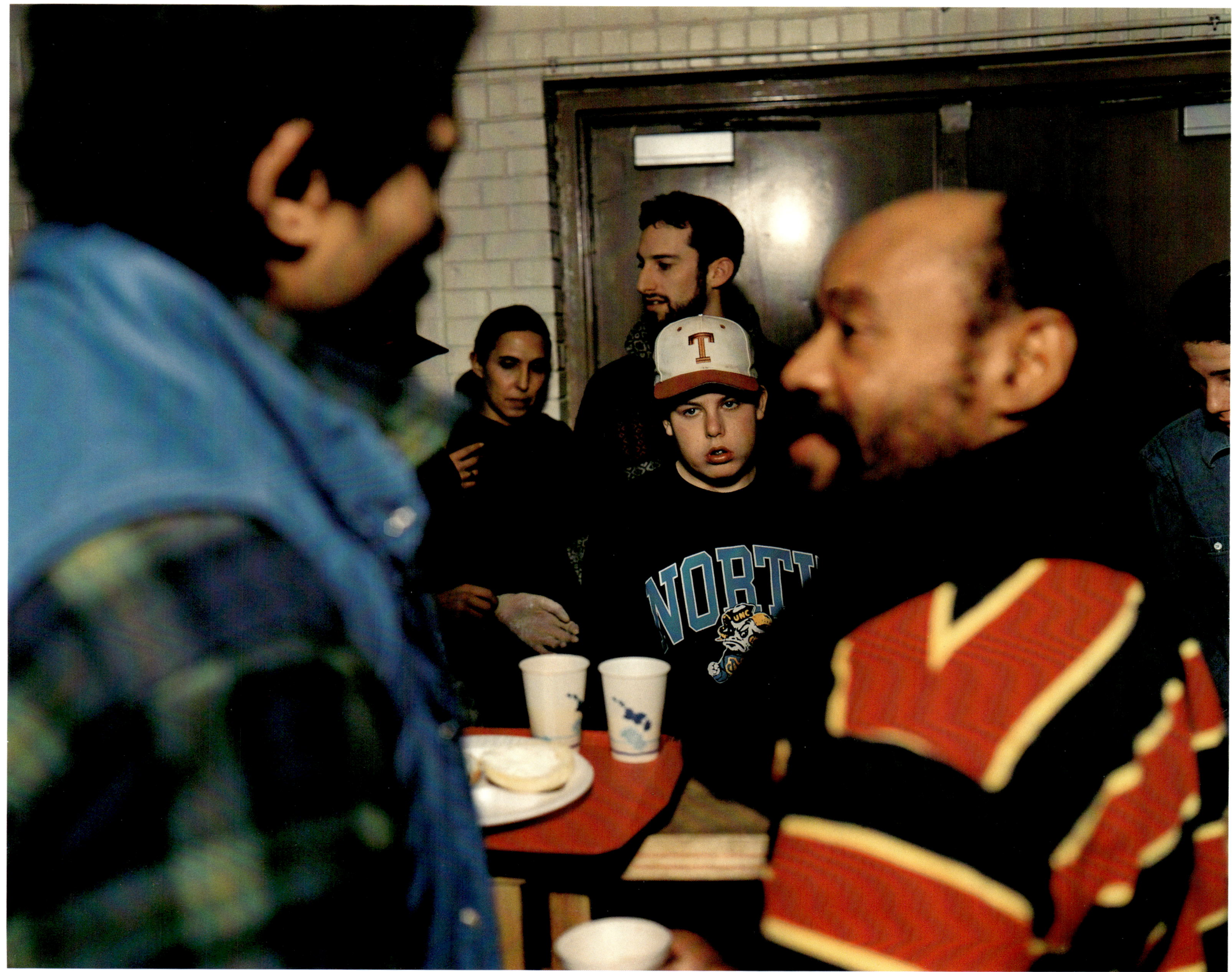

43 *Mitzvah Corps Serving Lunch, Christopher House,* Chicago, 1994

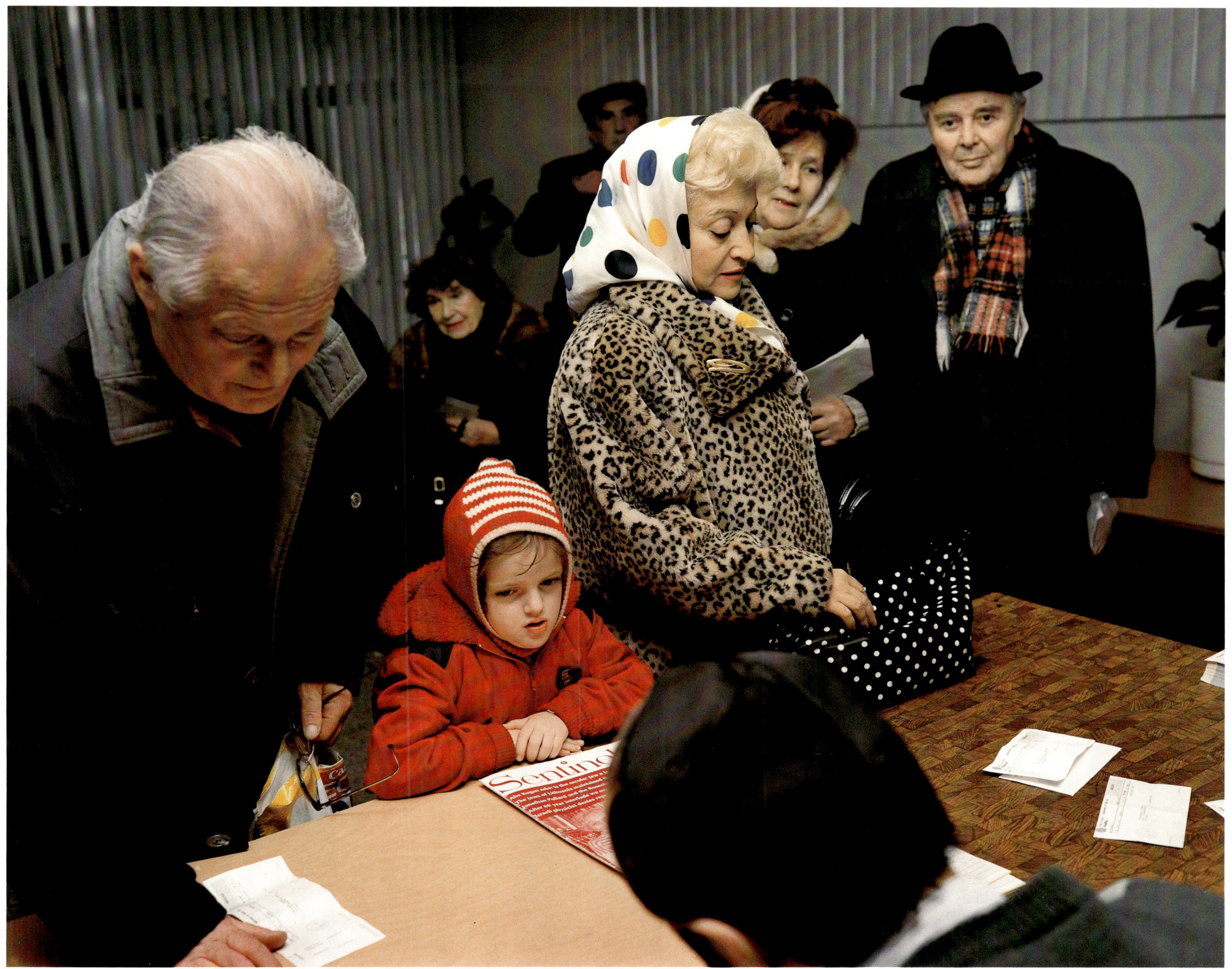

44 *Social Services for Russian Immigrants, Ark Social Service Center,* Chicago, 1993

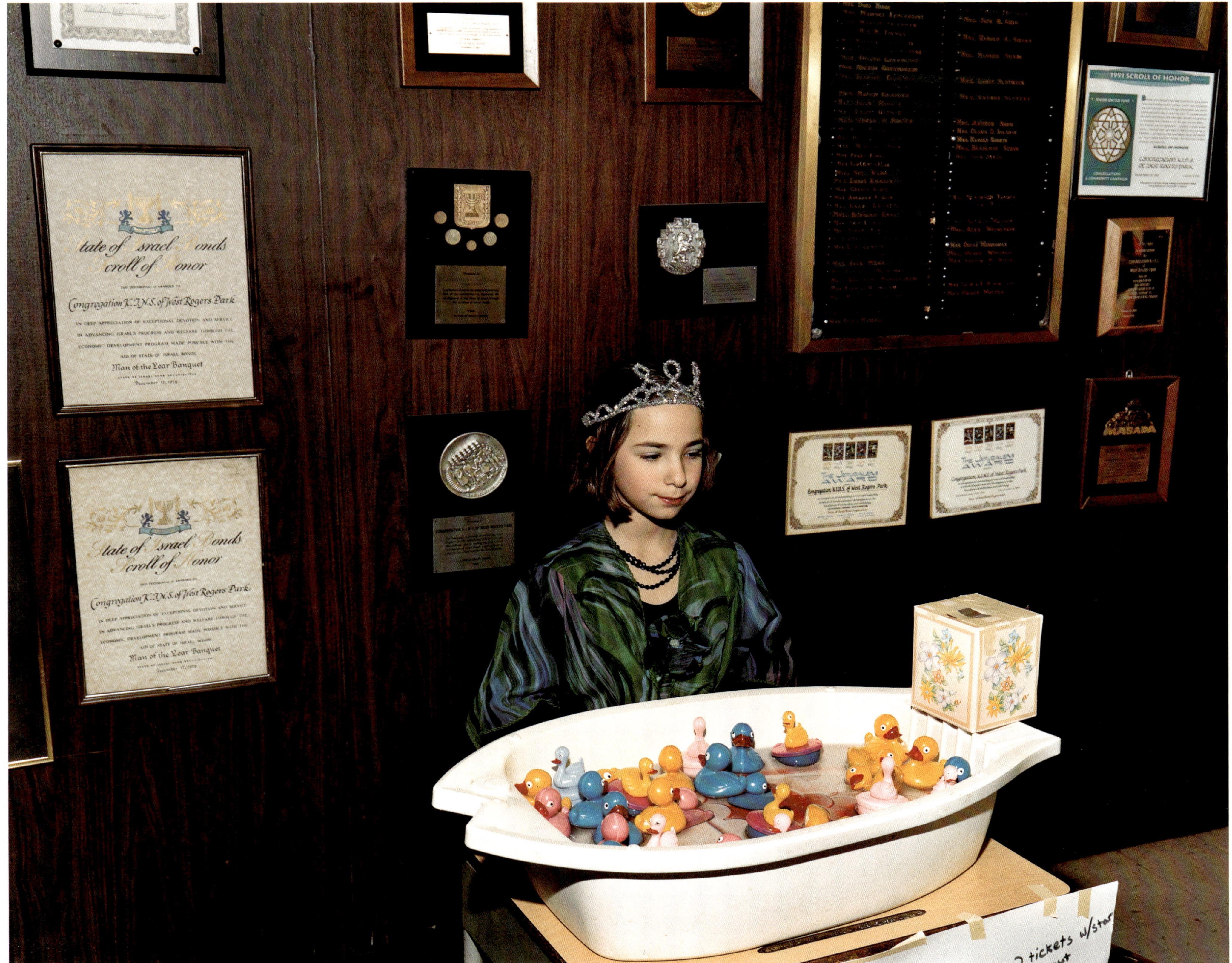

45 *Queen Esther, Purim Carnival, Congregation K.I.N.S.*, Chicago, 1993

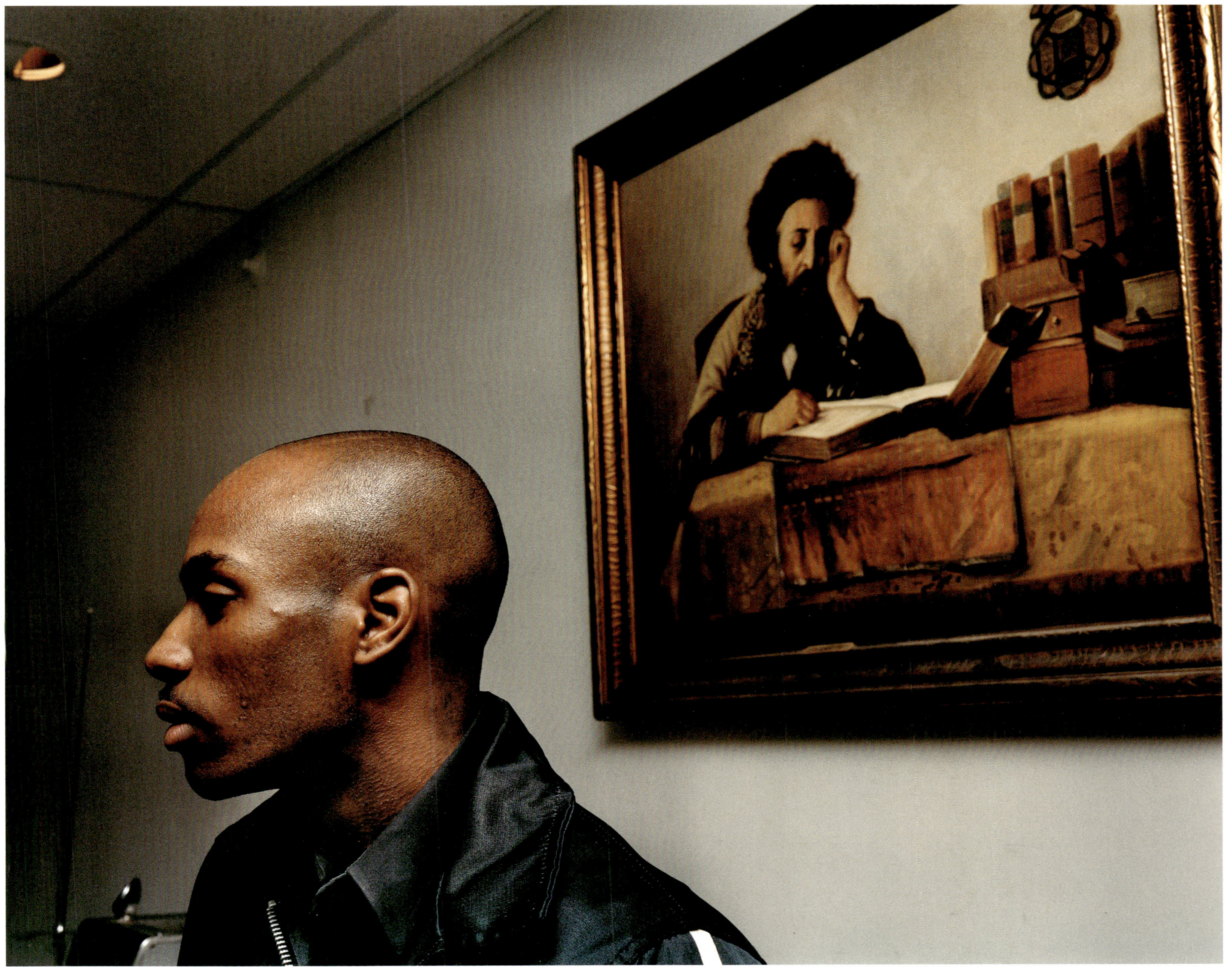

46 *Guard, Ark Social Service Center,* Chicago, 1993

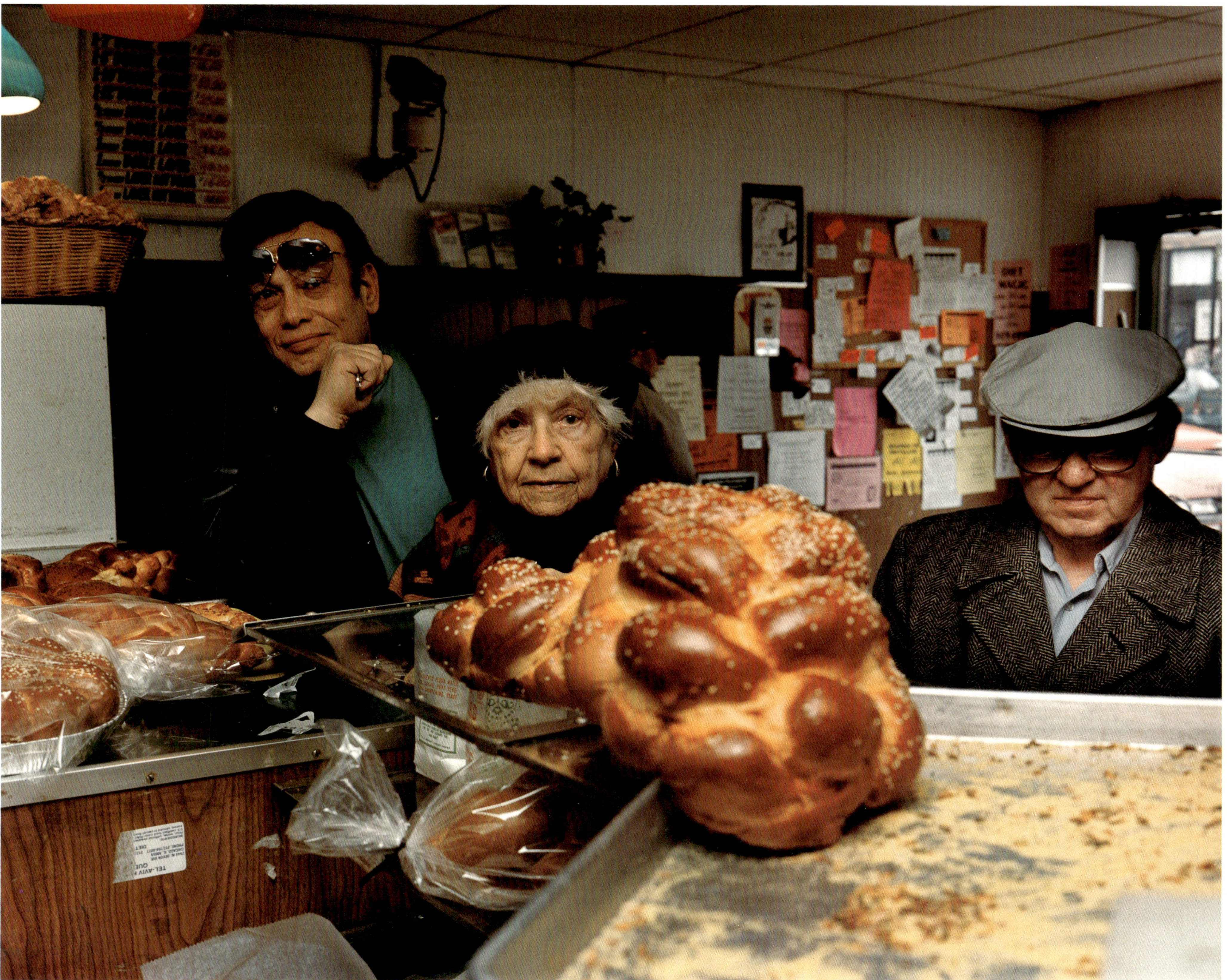

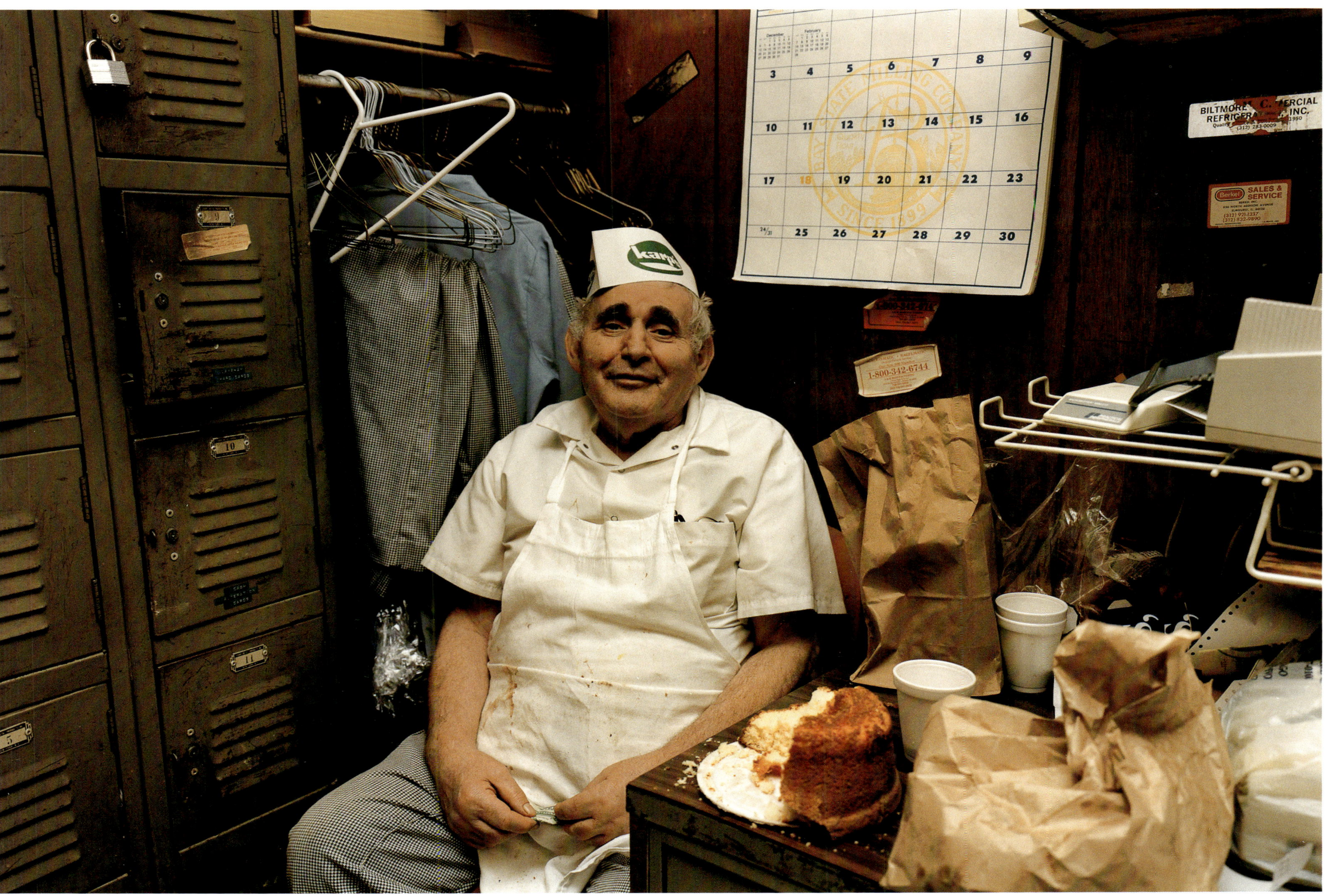

47 *Challah, Tel Aviv Bakery,* Chicago, 1993

48 *Baker, Tel Aviv Bakery,* Chicago, 1993

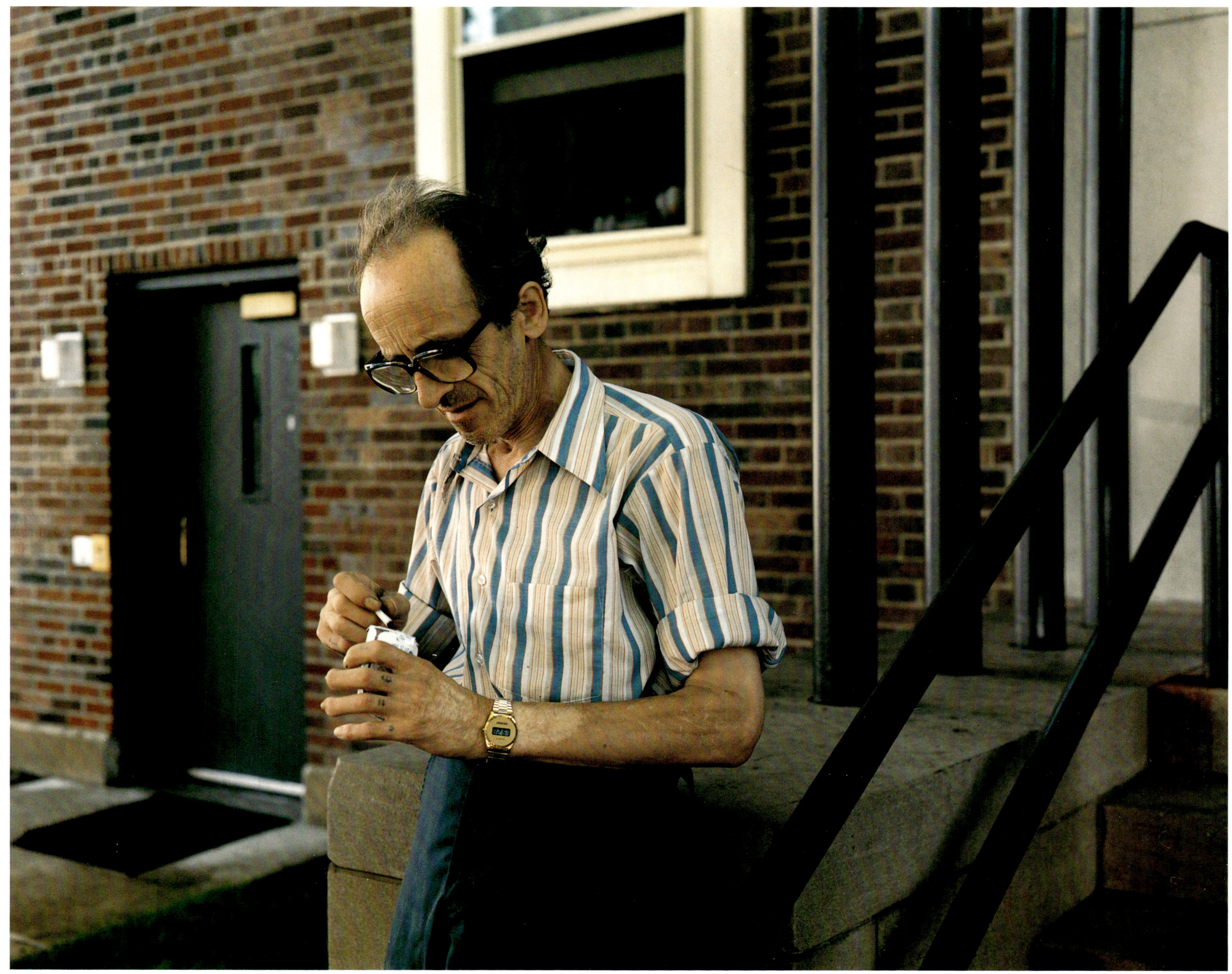

49 *Man from Odessa, Jewish Homeless Shelter,* Chicago, 1993

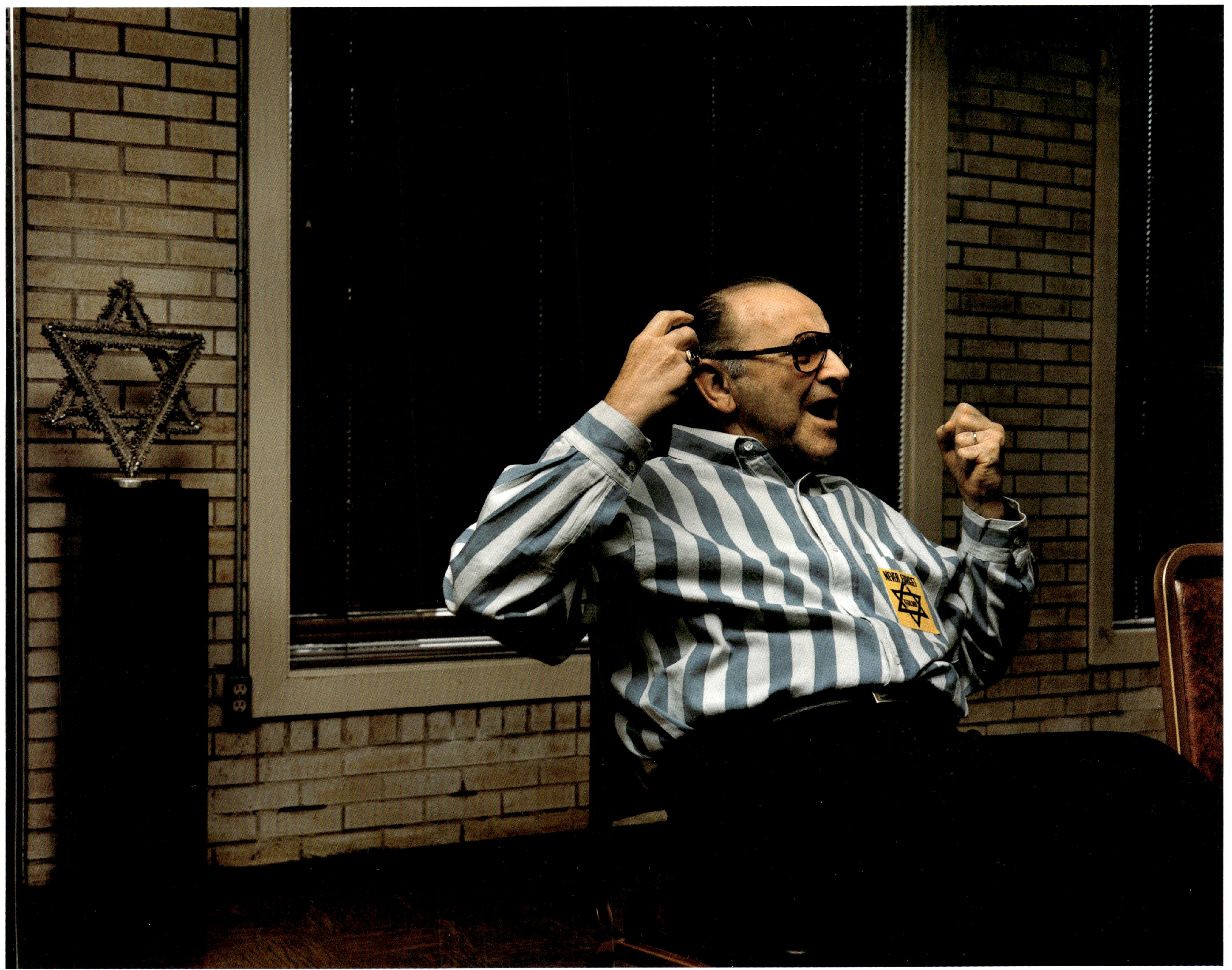

50 *Angry Man, Holocaust Day Discussion, Illinois Holocaust Memorial Foundation,* Skokie, Illinois, 1993

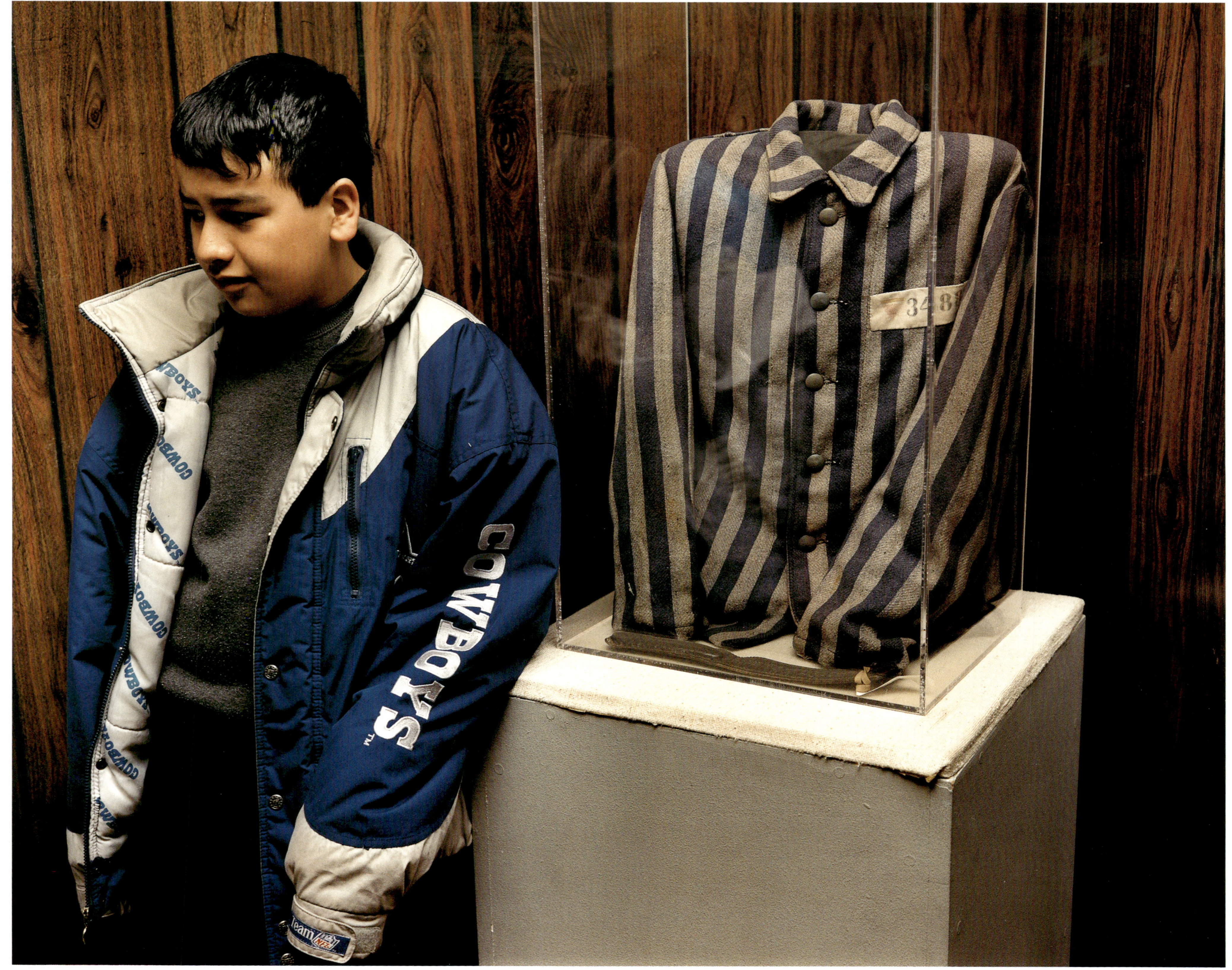

51 *Uniforms, Illinois Holocaust Memorial Foundation,* Skokie, Illinois, 1994

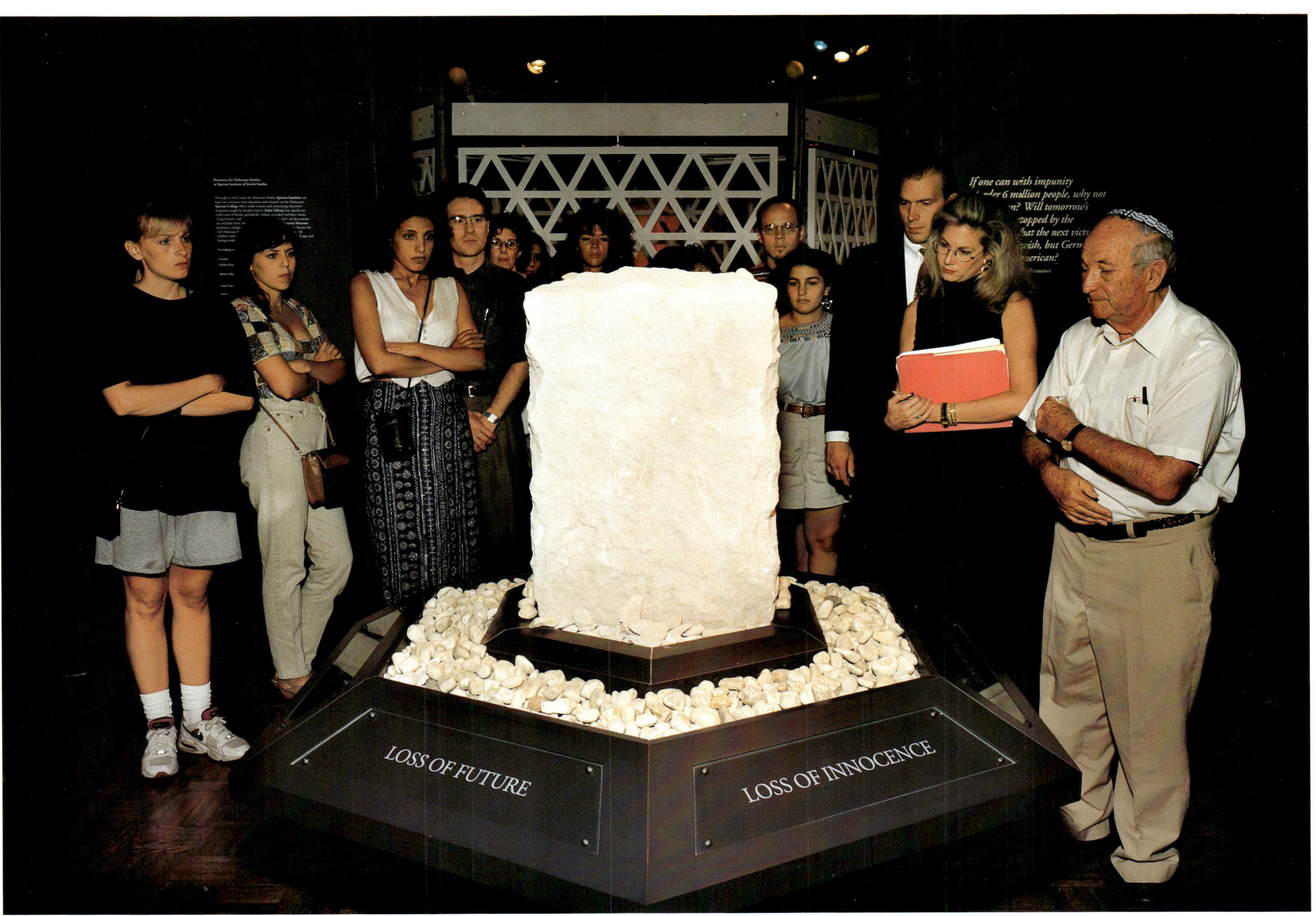

52 *Conversion Class, Holocaust Memorial, Spertus Institute,* Chicago, 1995

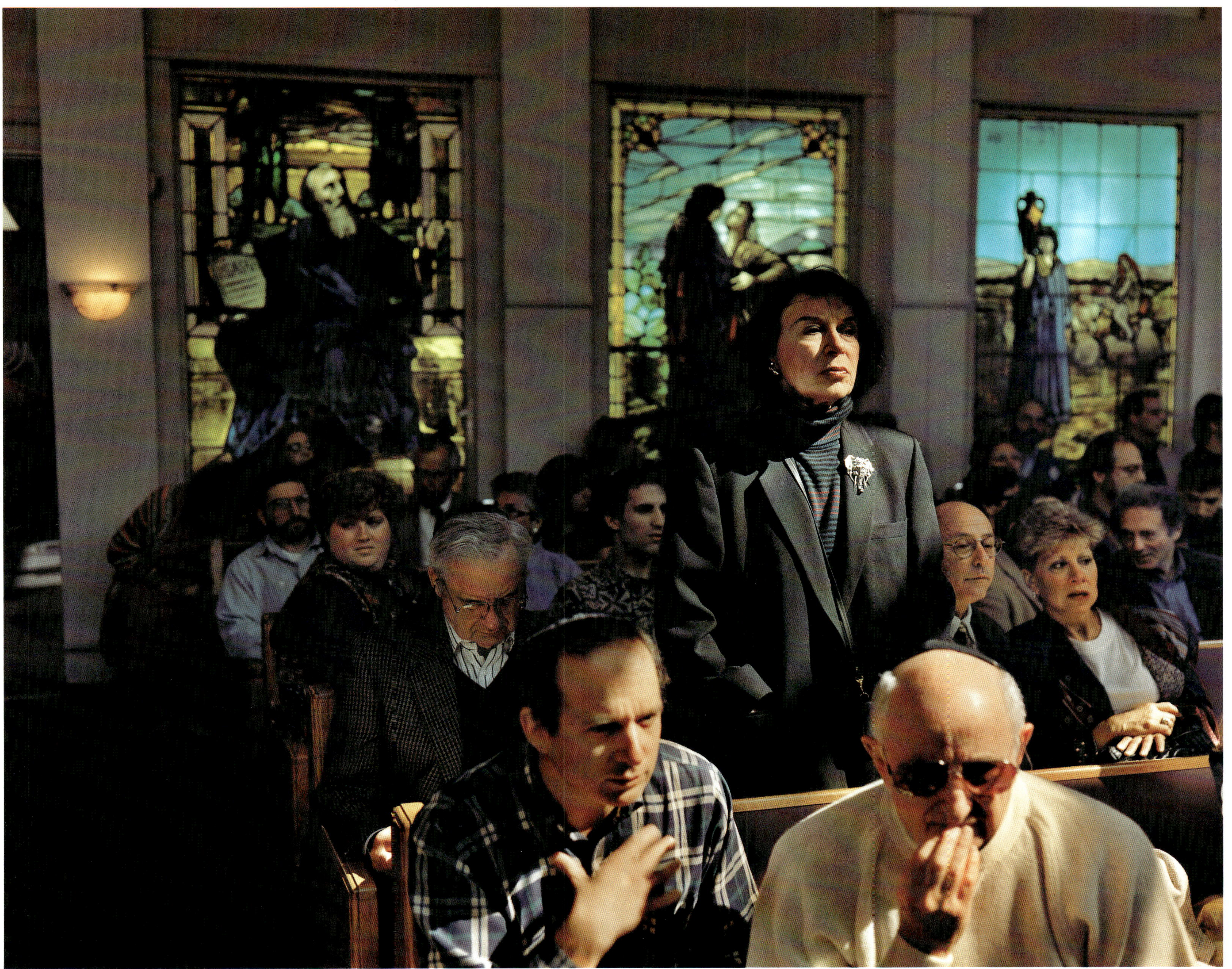

53 *Congregation, Before Elie Wiesel Lecture, Congregation Moriah,* Deerfield, Illinois, 1994

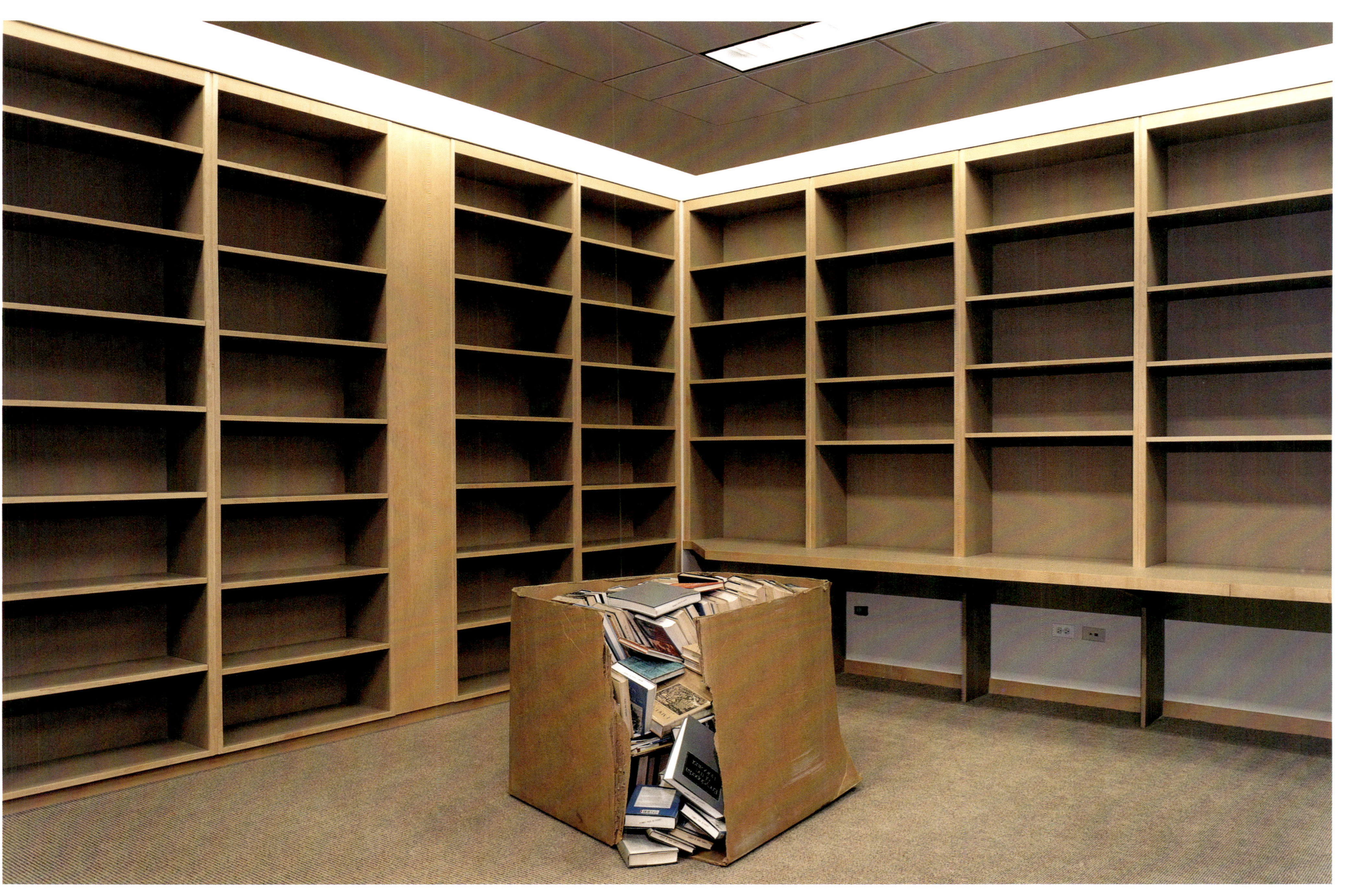

54 *Moving in, Library, Temple Sinai,* Chicago 1997

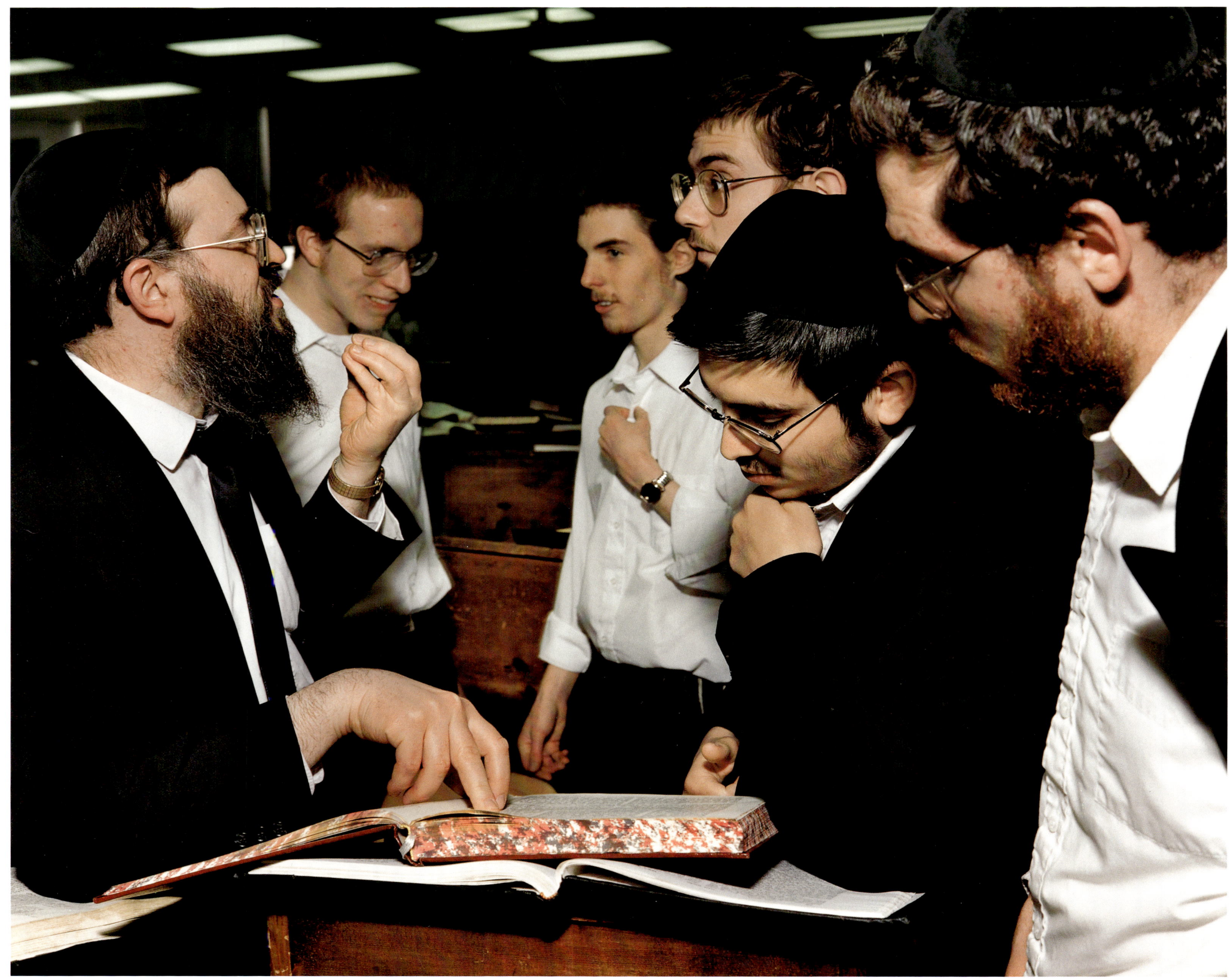

55 *Studying Talmud, Tels Yeshiva,* Chicago, 1995

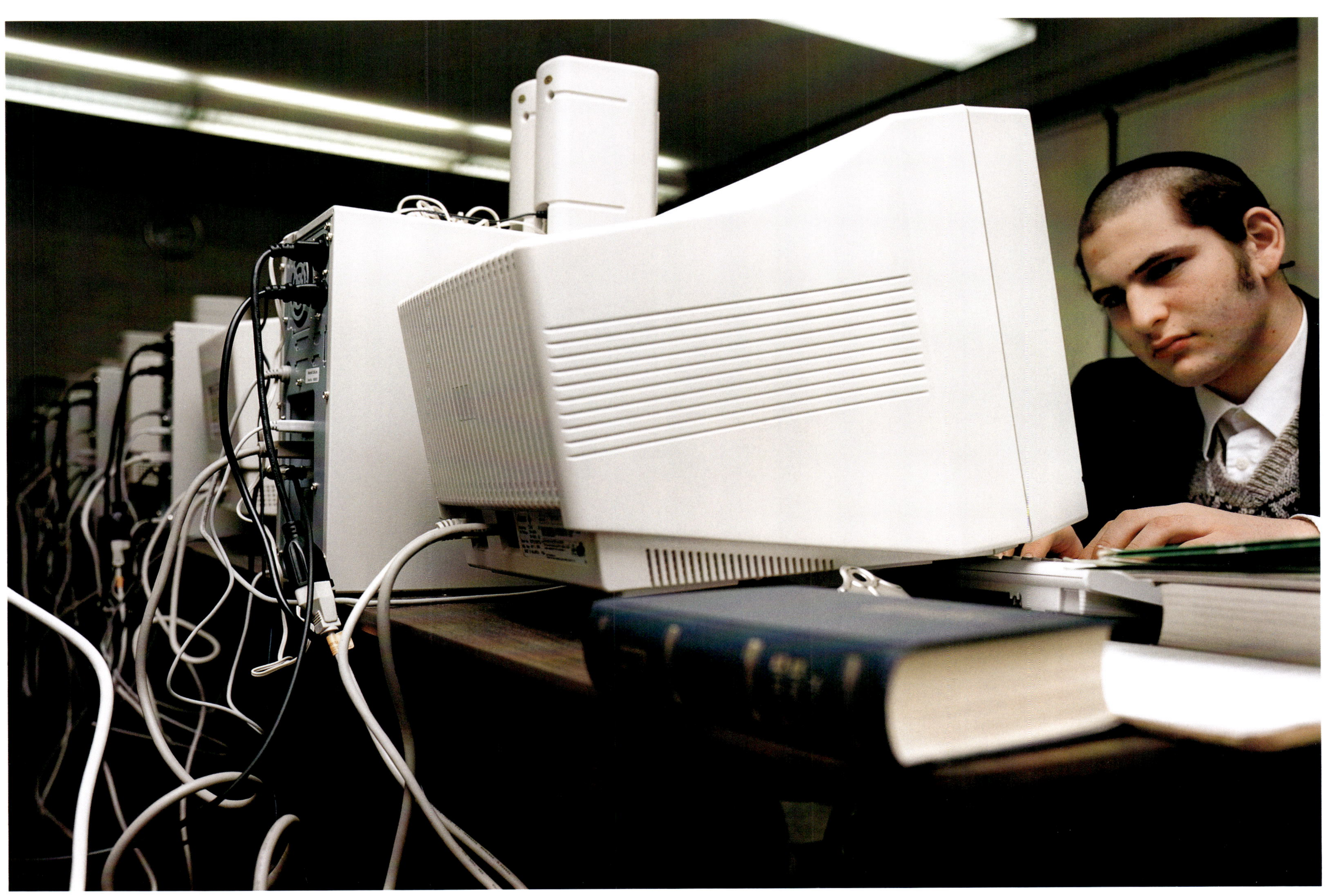

56 *Next Generation, Jewish Theological College,* Des Plaines, Illinois, 1996

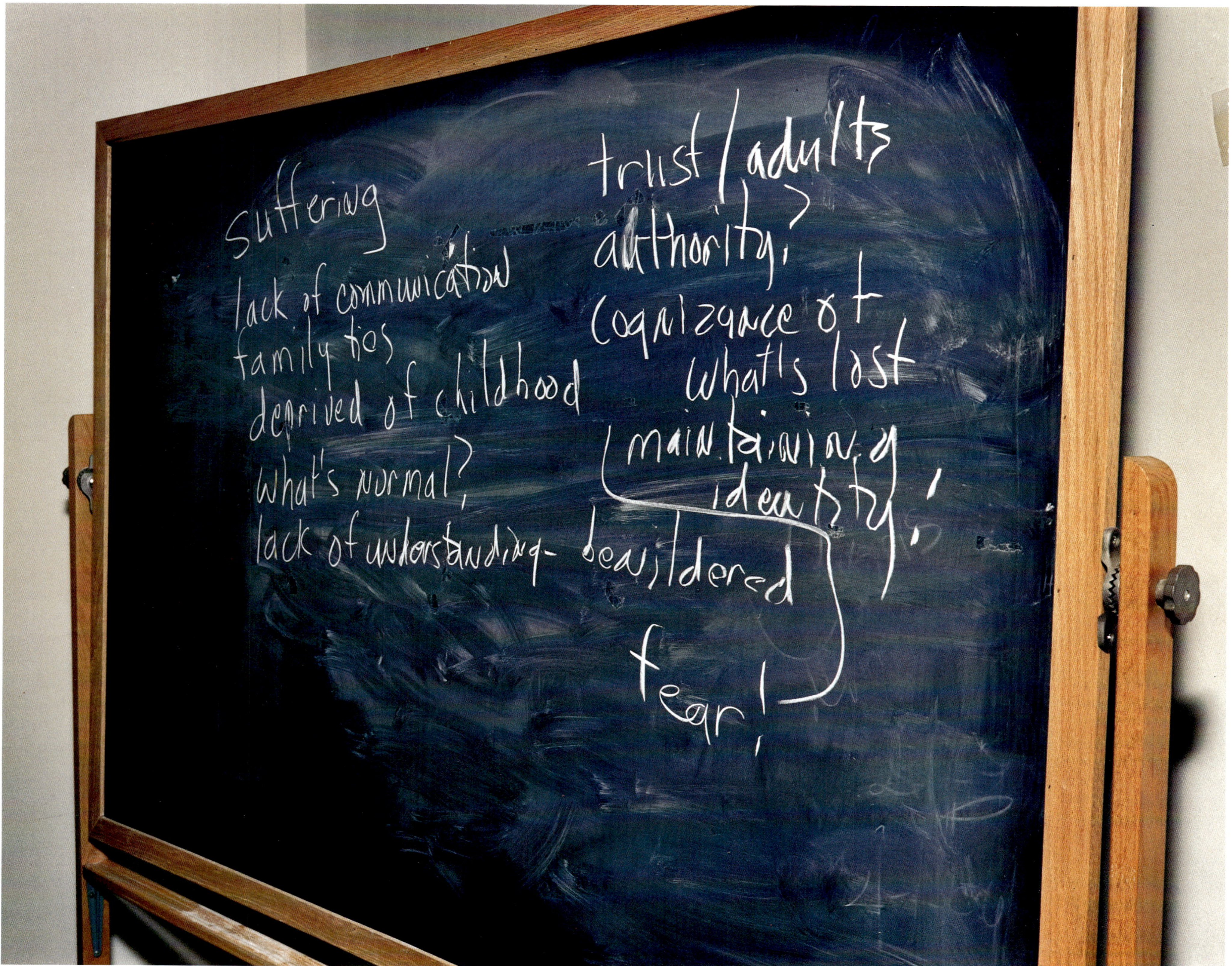

57 *Post-Lecture Blackboard, Child Holocaust Survivor, Illinois Holocaust Memorial Foundation,* Skokie, Illinois, 1994

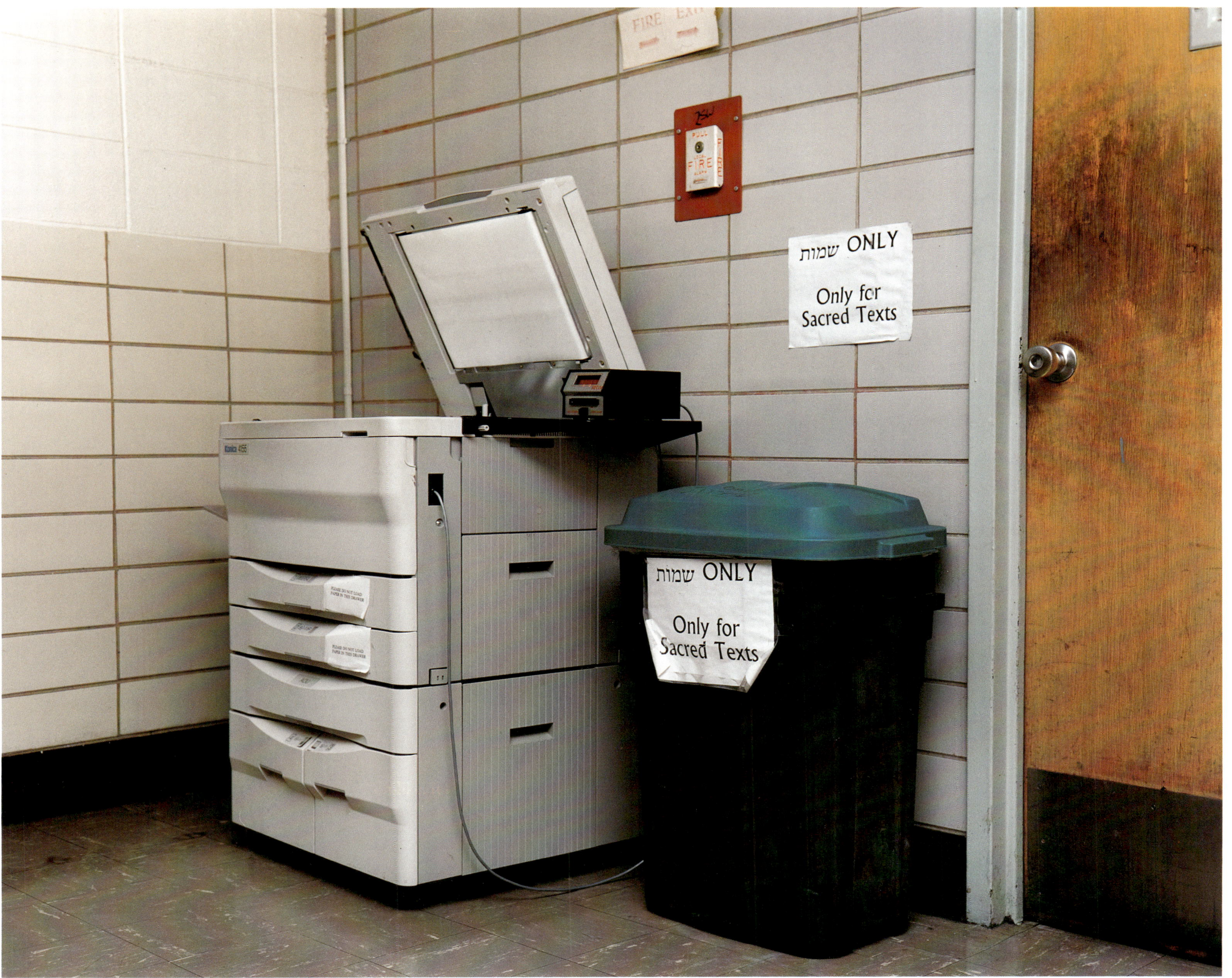

58 *Shemot (Names) Only, Jewish Theological College,* Des Plaines, Illinois, 1996

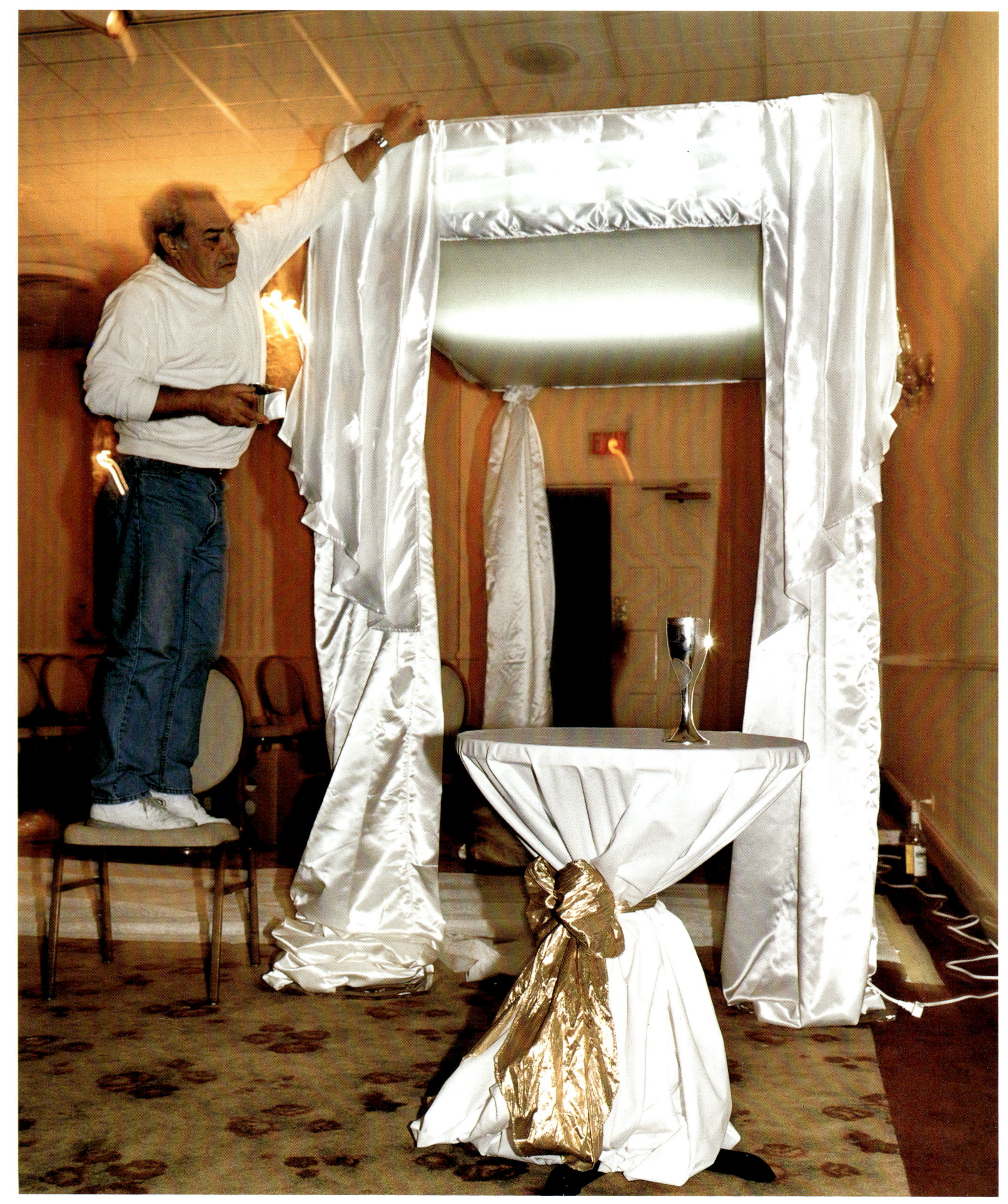

59 *Constructing Huppah, Iosevitch Wedding,* Highwood, Illinois, 1997

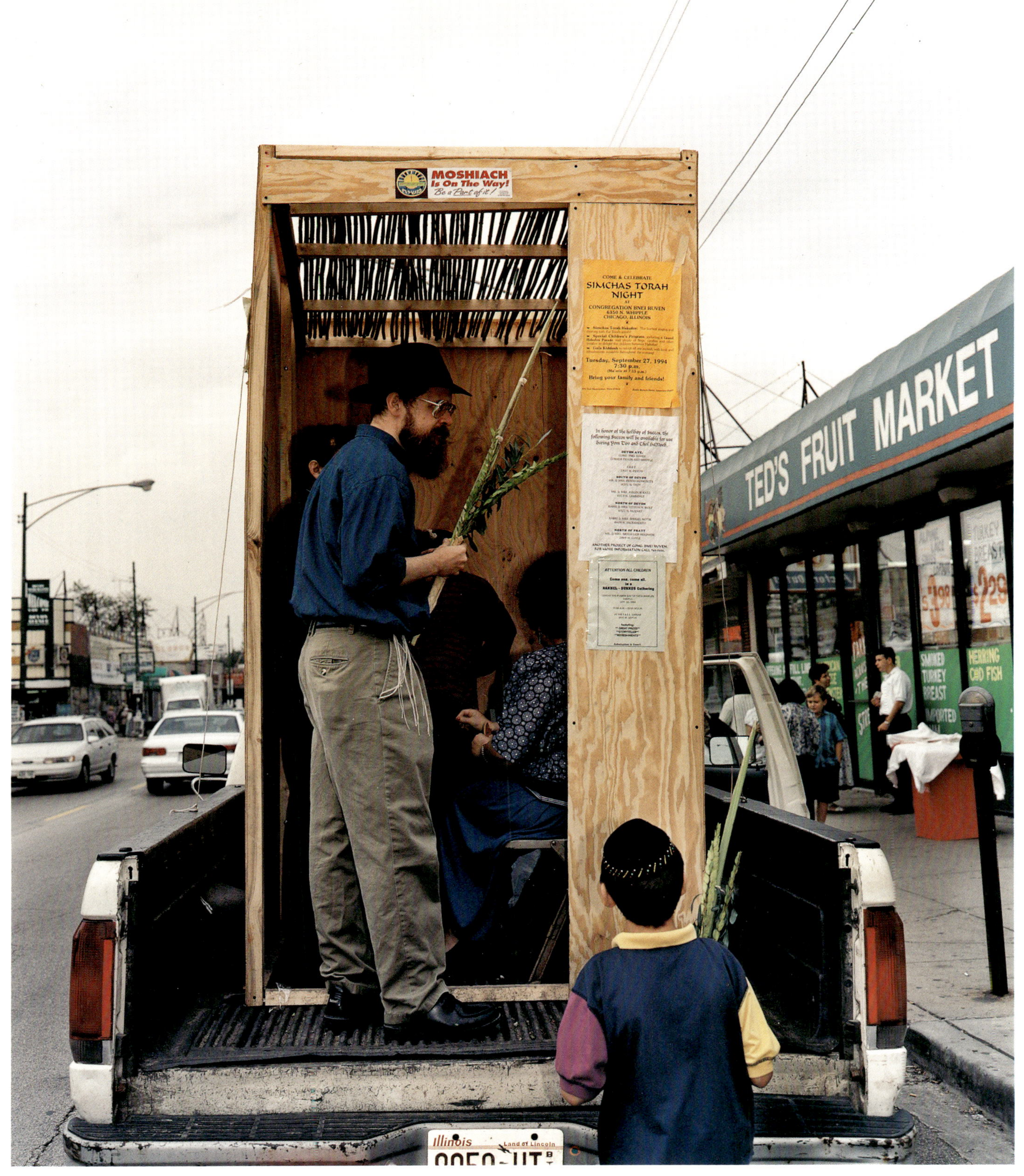

60 *Sukkah-Mobile, Devon Avenue,* Chicago, 1995

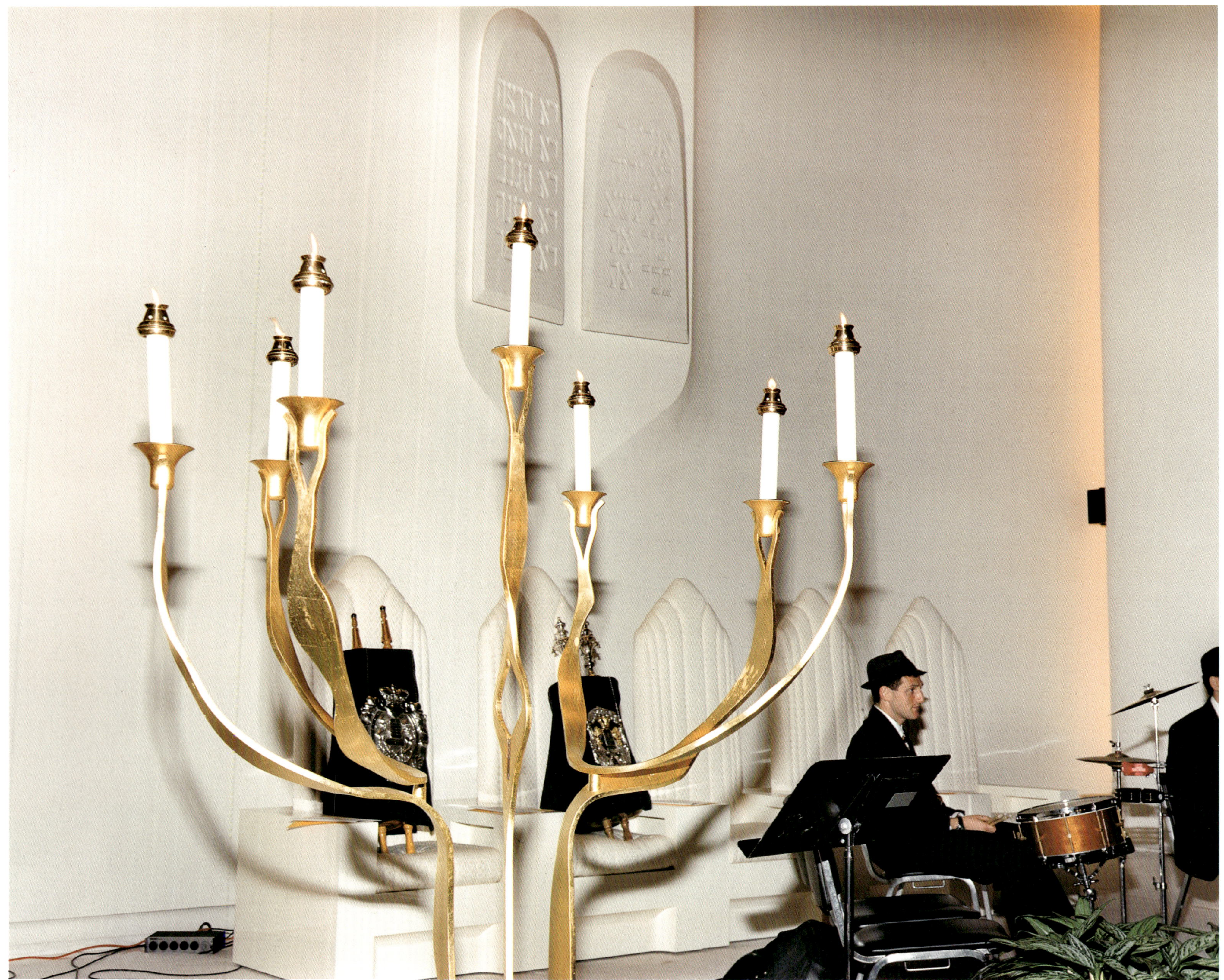

61 *Bimah Menorah, Drummer, North Shore Congregation Israel,* Glencoe, Illinois, 1994

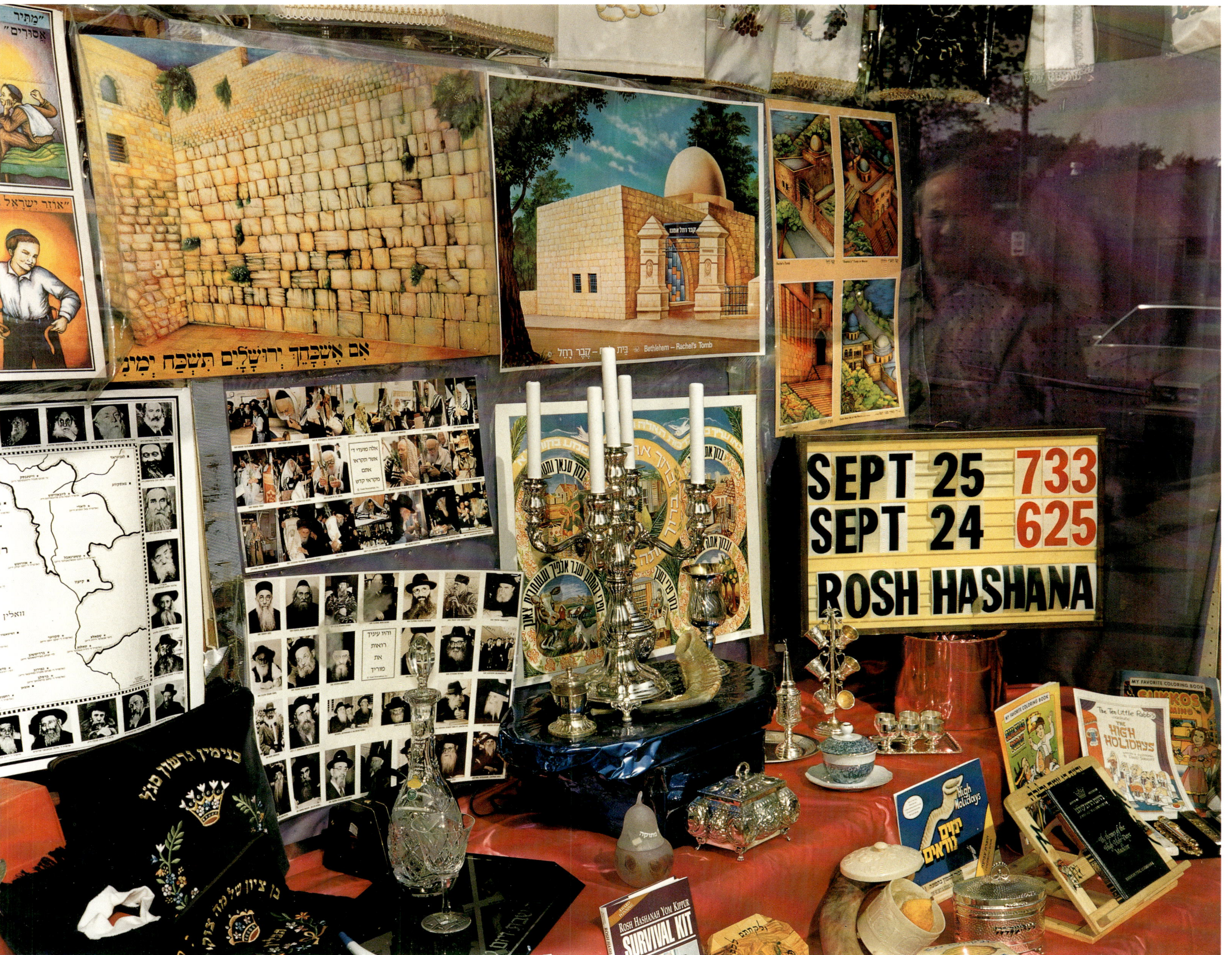

62 *Window, Chicago Hebrew Book Store, 1994*

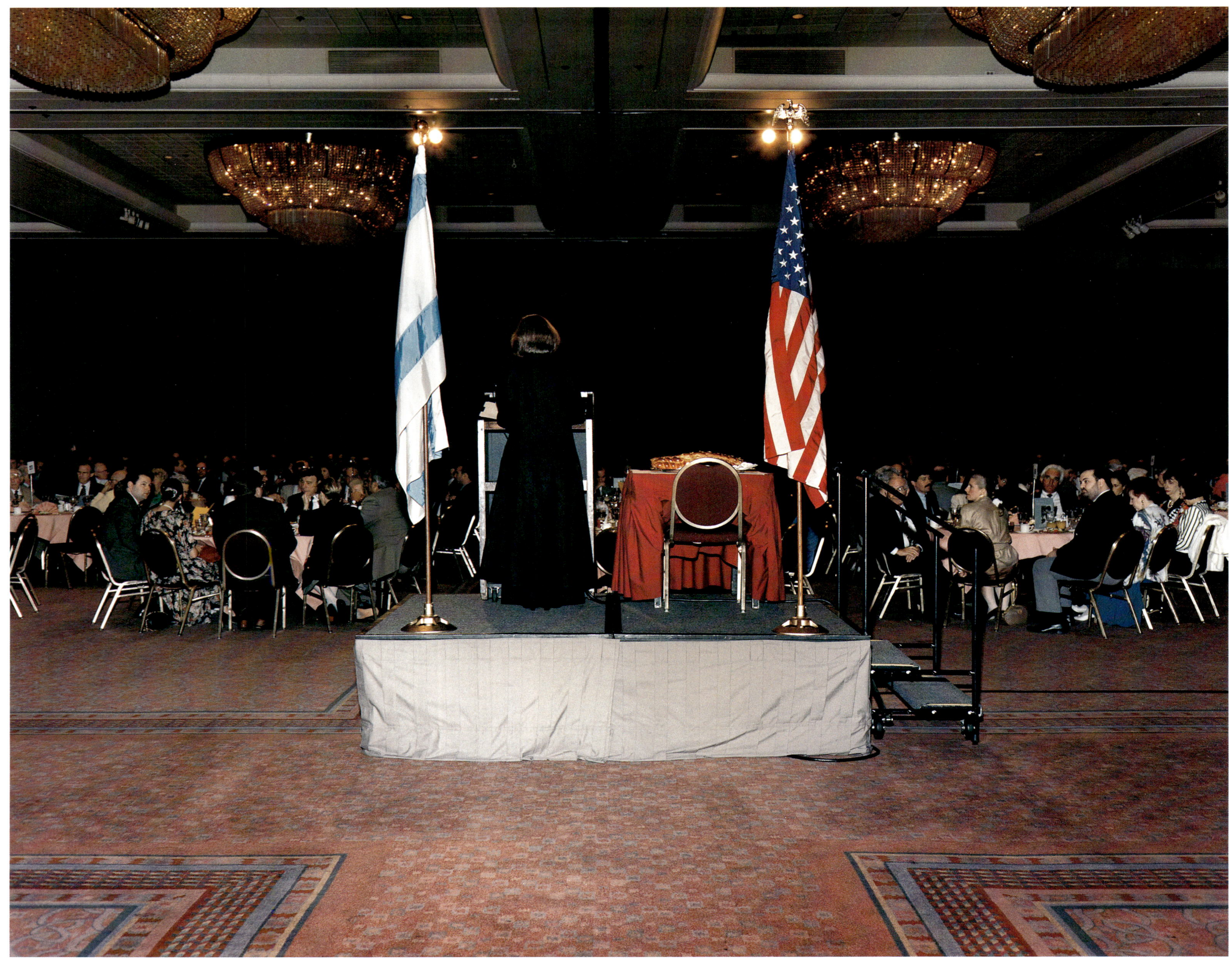

63 *Hamotzi (Blessing Over Bread), Jewish United Fund Dinner,* Chicago, 1994

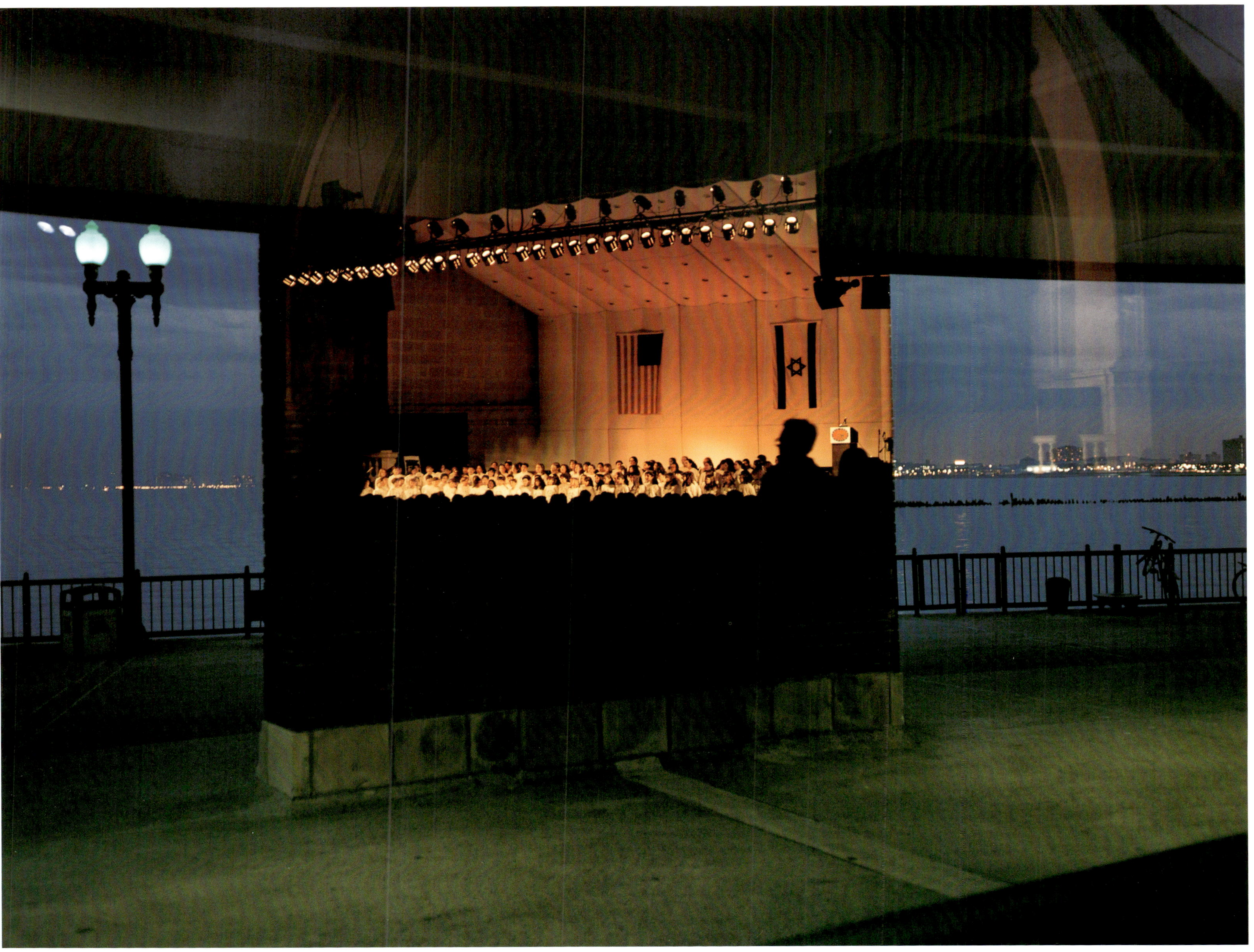

64 *Children's Chorus, Israel Independence Day Celebration, Navy Pier,* Chicago, 1994

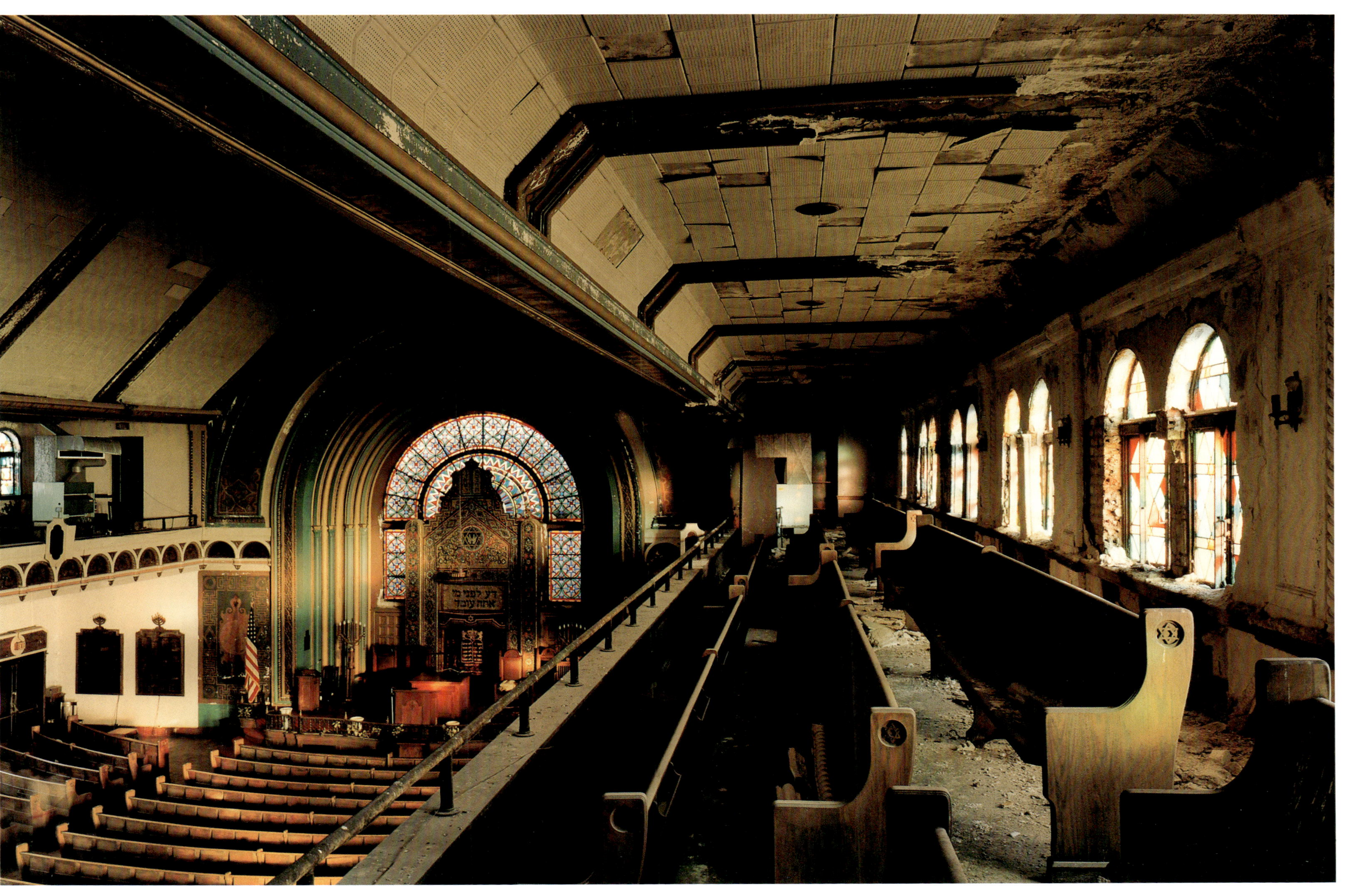

65 *Sanctuary, Congregation Agudas Achim,* Chicago, 1994

Explanatory Notes

Marshall Wolke

Plate 1
Da Lifnei Mi Atah Omed ("Know Before Whom You Stand"). An expression frequently inscribed over the reader's stand or over the Ark of the Covenant in a house of worship. It reminds the members of the congregation that they face the Almighty.

Plate 2
Chometz. Leaven in any substance that will cause flour to rise while baking. Because it is customary for Jews not to eat food containing leaven during Passover, *chometz* is burned on the evening before the festival begins.

Plate 3
Schlogging Kapparoth. A difficult expression, almost nonsensical in literal translation, that refers to the custom in which the sins of a person are symbolically transferred to a fowl as it is twirled overhead. This ceremony takes place the night before Yom Kippur eve, after which the fowl is given away to the poor.

Plate 4
Toyveling at the Mikvah. A ritual dipping of pots, pans, dishes, and utensils in the water of the ritual bath in order to make them kosher and fit for use in the Jewish home.

Plate 7
Bris; Elijah's Chair. The *bris,* or *brit millah,* is the ritual of circumcision that every Jewish boy must undergo on the eighth day of his life. One of the ceremonial objects of this ritual is the Chair of Elijah, a special place reserved for the prophet Elijah, who is "invited" to every *bris* as the guardian angel of babies.

Plate 8
Torah. The Pentateuch, or Five Books of Moses. It is read in the synagogue from a parchment scroll carefully inscribed by hand. Successive portions are read every Saturday so that the entire Torah is heard by the congregation within the year.

Shavuot. A major spring harvest festival that also commemorates the Jews' receiving of the Ten Commandments on Mount Sinai.

Plate 9
Beth Shalom B'Nai Zaken Ethiopian Congregation. A congregation of African-Americans who, in 1913, joined together as a community and converted to Judaism, which they practice to this day.

Plate 16
Burial, Burnt Torahs. Jewish tradition holds that when a Torah scroll or a sacred book is damaged, torn, burned, or desecrated, it is as though a life has been lost, and therefore the scroll or book must be buried in a Jewish cemetery.

Plate 18
Yellow Star. Under Nazi rule, every Jew in Germany was ordered to wear a yellow cloth scrap with the Star of David painted on it. The word *Jude* was often stenciled in the center.

Plate 19
Lag B'Omer. The Omer is a seven-week period lasting from the festival of Passover to the holiday of Shavuoth. During this time, Jews mark the Omer daily and observe a period of moderate mourning. The exception is Lag B'Omer—the thirty-third day of the Omer—when the restrictions are lifted, marriages are permitted, music may be played, and so on. It is usually a holiday for schoolchildren, who go on outings, engage in sports, and play games.

Plate 20
Sukkah. A booth erected for the fall festival of Sukkoth commemorating the shelters in which the Jews dwelt while traveling through the desert.

Plate 23
Seder. A feast held on Passover that commemorates the Jewish Exodus from slavery in ancient Egypt. The word *seder* means "order," which is significant because the feast and the accompanying chants telling the story of the Exodus follow a prescribed order that dates back to ancient times.

Congregation B'Nai Shalom. A congregation for the deaf in Chicago.

Plate 24
Chanukah. An eight-day festival commemorating the historic victory of the Maccabees over the Syrian tyrant Antiochus. Called the Festival of Lights, it celebrates the miracle of a small amount of oil burning for eight days in the reconquered and cleansed Second Temple of Jerusalem (see also notes for PL. 61).

Congregation Or Chadash ("New Light"). Formed in Chicago some years back to serve primarily the Jewish gay and lesbian community. Its services and practices are the same as those in other synagogues.

Plate 26
Bat Mitzvah. According to Jewish tradition, a girl reaches religious and legal maturity at age twelve plus one day (for boys it is age thirteen plus one day). At that point she is responsible for fulfilling all the commandments incumbent on an adult. A public celebration at the synagogue, called a Bat Mitzvah, marks the event (the celebration for boys is called a Bar Mitzvah).

Plate 27
Yeshiva. The boys in this photograph are enrolled in a yeshiva, a seminary where students engage in the study of holy texts. Jews believe that such continual study, searching, and examining of these texts are rewarding in their own right.

Plate 28
Performing for the Bride and Groom. At traditional Jewish weddings, the bride and groom sit at the table like a king and queen. Accordingly, they are entertained by actors, magicians, dancers, jesters, and others from their "court."

Plate 31
Women Watching, Men Dancing. A *mehitza* is a division in the synagogue used to separate men from women during public prayer. Similarly, at Orthodox weddings such a division separates male dancers from the female

dancers. It should be noted that the majority of dances at a wedding are not "ballroom"—they are folk dances, and are inspired by ritual.

Plate 32
Simhat Torah. A celebration of the Torah on the last day of the holiday begun as Sukkoth. This is the day when Jews finish the annual cycle of reading the Torah and immediately reroll the scroll to begin the next year's cycle. This celebration is accompanied by singing, dancing, and reading.

Plate 33
Badeken. A custom followed by traditional Jews in which the groom is "led" to visit the bride in her "suite" prior to the wedding. When assured that the woman before him is indeed his betrothed, he pulls a veil over her face, and then the bride is led to the wedding canopy.

Plate 34
Post-Yom Kippur Singles Dance. A modern custom in which, after twenty-four hours of fasting and prayers on the Day of Atonement, young people gather to meet, dance, and enjoy the post-fast mood.

Plate 38
Tisha B'Av. The ninth day of the Jewish month of Av, which traditionally is believed to be the day on which both the First and Second Temples were destroyed. Legend has it that many other disasters that befell the Jewish people took place on this day.

Plate 43
Mitzvah Corps. The word *mitzvah,* roughly translated, means "good deed"; *mitzvot* are literally the six hundred thirteen commandments prescribed in the Old Testament. The Mitzvah Corps is a group of high school and college students, sponsored by the Jewish Council on Urban Affairs, who perform *mitzvot* such as feeding the homeless and giving assistance to congregations and individuals in need of help.

Plate 44
Ark Social Service Center. The Ark is one of the many philanthropic agencies of the Jewish Federation. From its inception, it served the needy in the Jewish community with meals, clothing, furniture, medical and legal advice, and a variety of public services.

Plate 45
Purim. A festival of redemption that celebrates the Jews' survival against the Persian King Ahasuerus and his wicked viceroy Haman. The Jewish Queen Esther, alerted by her uncle Mordecai, prevented the slaughter of the Jews from taking place. It is customary on Purim for children and adults to dress in costume, eat special foods, and celebrate with carnivals and revelry.

Plate 47
Challah. A loaf of egg-rich bread braided into twelve knots that represent the Twelve Tribes of Israel. Challah is the bread served at Sabbath and holiday meals.

Plate 55
Talmud. The name applied to the great compilations in which are collected the teachings of the major Jewish scholars who flourished during the classic period of Rabbinic Judaism (200 to 800 B.C.).

Plate 58
Shemot. The Hebrew name for the Book of Exodus, second book of the Torah. Also, the variations of the names of the Almighty or other sacred names. According to Orthodox practice, any text (original or reproduced) containing *shemot* that is going to be discarded must be buried in the same way as a damaged Torah (see notes for PL. 16).

Plate 59
Huppah. The wedding canopy under which a Jewish bride and groom take their vows. The canopy is held up by four posts. This word is also used for the actual marriage ceremony.

Plate 60
Sukkah-Mobile. A vehicle brought by the Chabad Hasidic movement to public places (often in universities) to give people an opportunity to observe the *mitzvah* of "sitting" in a *sukkah* and to bless symbols of Sukkoth (the *lulav* and the *ethrog*).

Moshiach. In this photograph, the word *Moshiach* ("Messiah") appears at the top of the Sukkah-Mobile. Rabbinic doctrine and prophetic teaching say that the Messiah will come to reestablish the Davidic Dynasty in a newly rebuilt Temple in Jerusalem.

Plate 61
Bimah. Raised platform in the synagogue from which the Torah is read, and on which the rabbi and cantor stand as they lead the service.

Menorah. The seven-branched candelabrum that once stood in the Holy Temple. Its origin can be traced to the portable sanctuary (the tabernacle) in the wilderness. This symbolic object, which can also have nine branches, holds the candles that are ritually lit for Chanukah.

Checklist

All images were made with 6-by-7-cm and 6-by-9-cm rangefinder cameras on color negative films. Exhibition prints have been made on 16-by-20-inch and 20-by-24-inch Ektacolor Type C materials.

Frontispiece
Men Dancing, Sukkoth Celebration, Yeshiva Migdal Torah, Chicago, 1993

1
Da Lifnei Mi Atah Omed (Know Before Whom You Stand), Sanctuary, Congregation Agudas Achim, Chicago, 1994

2
Burning Chometz Before Passover, Chicago, 1993

3
Schlogging Kapporoth Before Yom Kippur, Chicago, 1994

4
Toyveling at the Mikvah, Chicago, 1995

5
Sanctuary Construction, Temple Sinai, Chicago, 1997

6
Baby in Hallway, Jewish Homeless Shelter, Chicago, 1994

7
Steve's Bris, Elijah's Chair, Deerfield, Illinois, 1996

8
Torah Reading, Shavuot, Congregation Etz Haim, Camp Beber, Mukwonago,Wisconsin, 1997

9
Torah Reading, Beth Shalom B'Nai Zaken Ethiopian Congregation, Chicago, 1994

10
Boys, Morning Service, Ida Crown Academy, Chicago, 1993

11
Evening Service, Westin O'Hare Lobby, Rosemont, Illinois, 1997

12
Friday Evening Sabbath Service, North Shore Congregation Israel, Glencoe, Illinois, 1995

13
Burnt Prayer Books, Post-Arson Fire, F.R.E.E. (Friends of Refugees of Eastern Europe) Congregation, Chicago, 1993

14
Public Rally, Post-Arson Fire, F.R.E.E. (Friends of Refugees of Eastern Europe) Congregation, Chicago, 1993

15
Mourning Burnt Torahs, Post-Arson Fire, F.R.E.E. (Friends of Refugees of Eastern Europe) Congregation, Chicago, 1993

16
Burial, Burnt Torahs, Post-Arson Fire, F.R.E.E. (Friends of Refugees of Eastern Europe) Congregation, Waldheim Cemetery, Forest Park, Illinois, 1993

17
Barbed-Wire Star, Camp Beber, Mukwonago, Wisconsin, 1997

18
Running Away, Yellow Star Stencil, Chicago, 1994

19
Lag B'Omer Festival, Horwich J.C.C., Chicago, 1993

20
Sukkah, Chicago Loop Synagogue, 1994

21
Men in the Sukkah, Chicago Loop Synagogue, 1995

22
Half-Time Prayer, Regional High School Basketball Finals, Chicago, 1996

23
Passover Seder in American Sign Language, Congregation B'Nai Shalom, Chicago, 1995

24
Chanukah Candle Lighting, Congregation Or Chadash, Chicago, 1995

25
Recreation Hall, Camp Ramah, Rhinelander, Wisconsin, 1994

26
Boxers, Whitney's Bat Mitzvah, Kenilworth, Illinois, 1994

27
Boys Dancing, Sukkoth Celebration, Yeshiva Migdal Torah, Chicago, 1993

28
Performing for the Bride and Groom, Spirn Wedding, Chicago, 1997

29
Mouths, Sukkoth Celebration, Migdal Torah, Chicago, 1993

30
Father and Son, Chanukah Celebration, Congregation B'Nai Tikvah, Deerfield, Illinois, 1995

31
Women Watching, Men Dancing, Spirn Wedding, Rosemont, Illinois, 1997

32
Simhat Torah, North Shore Congregation Israel, Glencoe, Illinois, 1994

33
Badeken (Veiling), Spirn Wedding, Chicago, 1997

34
Post-Yom Kippur Singles Dance, Lincolnwood, Illinois, 1993

35
Communal Seder, Man, Two Women, Chicago, 1993

36
Conversation, Whitney's Bat Mitzvah, Kenilworth, Illinois, 1994

37
Cultural Presentation, Ida Crown Academy, Chicago, 1994

38
Pro-Israel Demonstration, Tisha B'Av, Chicago, 1995

39
Girls, Morning Service, Ida Crown Academy, Chicago, 1994

40
Girls in Hallway, Ida Crown Academy, Chicago, 1995

41
Meeting, Concerned Women for Israeli Security, Chicago, 1995

42
Father and Son, Chanukah Preparation, Congregation Rodfei Zedek, Chicago, 1994

43
Mitzvah Corps Serving Lunch, Christopher House, Chicago, 1994

44
Social Services for Russian Immigrants, Ark Social Service Center, Chicago, 1993

45
Queen Esther, Purim Carnival, Congregation K.I.N.S., Chicago, 1993

46
Guard, Ark Social Service Center, Chicago, 1993

47
Challah, Tel Aviv Bakery, Chicago, 1993

48
Baker, Tel Aviv Bakery, Chicago, 1993

49
Man from Odessa, Jewish Homeless Shelter, Chicago, 1993

50
Angry Man, Holocaust Day Discussion, Illinois Holocaust Memorial Foundation, Skokie, Illinois, 1993

51
Uniforms, Illinois Holocaust Memorial Foundation, Skokie, Illinois, 1994

52
Conversion Class, Holocaust Memorial, Spertus Institute, Chicago, 1995

53
Congregation, Before Elie Wiesel Lecture, Congregation Moriah, Deerfield, Illinois, 1994

54
Moving in, Library, Temple Sinai, Chicago, 1997

55
Studying Talmud, Tels Yeshiva, Chicago, 1995

56
Next Generation, Jewish Theological College, Des Plaines, Illinois, 1996

57
Post-Lecture Blackboard, Child Holocaust Survivor, Illinois Holocaust Memorial Foundation, Skokie, Illinois, 1994

58
Shemot (Names) Only, Jewish Theological College, Des Plaines, Illinois, 1996

59
Constructing Huppah, Iosevitch Wedding, Highwood, Illinois, 1997

60
Sukkah-Mobile, Devon Avenue, Chicago, 1995

61
Bimah Menorah, Drummer, North Shore Congregation Israel, Glencoe, Illinois, 1994

62
Window, Chicago Hebrew Book Store, 1994

63
Hamotzi (Blessing Over Bread), Jewish United Fund Dinner, Chicago, 1994

64
Children's Chorus, Israel Independence Day Celebration, Navy Pier, Chicago, 1994

65
Sanctuary, Congregation Agudas Achim, Chicago, 1994

Acknowledgments

I wish to thank my parents, Marshall and Estelle Wolke, who instilled in me a respect and love of Jewish life, the knowledge and perspective to coexist in an American culture, and the courage and commitment to communicate my views to others.

I must express immeasurable thanks and love to my wife, Avril Greenberg, for her constant humor, patience, and unfailing advice during the six years of this project. Her gifts have ensured my joy, my humility, and my humanity.

My great appreciation goes to David Travis, who, through mutual respect and friendship, gave me the vision and confidence to make this book and exhibition a reality. His curatorial expertise has facilitated this entire project. Additionally, I must thank Jim Iska and the entire staff of the Art Institute's Department of Photography for their tremendous assistance and their regard for my work.

My admiration and thanks go to Joel Snyder, who, over the years, has championed my photographs, provided me with countless insights, and opened his soul and his enormous intellect to write the essay for this publication.

I must acknowledge the tremendous support and commitment of Susan F. Rossen, Michael Sittenfeld, Amanda Freymann, and the rest of the staff of the Art Institute's Publications Department. I am fortunate to have been the beneficiary of their unparalleled professionalism and concern for excellence.

I am also tremendously grateful to James N. Wood, Director and President of the Art Institute, who understood this project as a valuable link to the community at large and, to that end, dedicated the extensive resources of the museum to the exhibition and this catalogue.

When this publication was only a pipe dream, a number of individuals had the vision to commit funding and support. My unqualified thanks go to Jack Jaffe, the David and Sarajean Ruttenberg Foundation, Sonia and Ted Bloch, Arnold Thaler, Mr. and Mrs. Richard S. Press, Mr. and Mrs. Ralph Segall, Judd Malkin, Neil Bluhm, Terry Lallak and Susan Tom, Ruth Horwich, the Weinberg Family Foundation, the Reva and David Logan Foundation, and Joel and Esther Mosak.

Of the thousands of photographs made for this project, only a small fraction are represented in this book and in the exhibition. I would like to thank the innumerable subjects, congregations, and facilitators who advised me, made connections, and allowed me into their lives to shoot candidly and without censorship. As this has been a generative process, I must acknowledge the extreme value of everyone's participation, without which this project would never have been realized.

Life support: Harold Allen, Tom Arndt, Richard Block, Patty Carroll, Bea Colbourn, Paul D'Amato, Tony D'Orio, Jack Jaffe, Wendy Katz, Cliff Kavinsky, Jim Linehan, Denise Miller, Naomi Stern, and Joe and Barb Wolke.

Finally, I am deeply grateful to my many other close friends, my wonderful family both near and far, as well as my teachers, colleagues, and students at the Institute of Design. Each one has taught me something unique and invaluable.

Jay Wolke

Notes on Contributors

Joel Snyder is Professor in the Department of Art History at the University of Chicago. He has written extensively about the history and theory of photography and on topics centering on the use of linear perspective. Snyder has been an editor of the academic journal *Critical Inquiry* since 1981.

David Travis has been Curator of Photography at The Art Institute of Chicago since 1972. He has curated or cocurated many exhibitions for the Art Institute and other institutions, including "Brassaï and Company" (1998), "Moholy-Nagy and Present Company" (1995), "On the Art of Fixing a Shadow" (1989), "The Photography of Gustave Le Gray" (1987), and "André Kertész: Of Paris and New York" (1985), and has published numerous essays on the history of photography and on contemporary photographers.

Jay Wolke is Coordinator of Graduate Studies in Documentary Photography at the Institute of Design, Illinois Institute of Technology, in Chicago. Exhibitions of his work have been held at Harvard University, the Museum of Contemporary Photography in Chicago, the Chicago Historical Society, and other museums and galleries. His work is in the collections of the Museum of Modern Art, the Brooklyn Museum of Art, and The Art Institute of Chicago.

Marshall Wolke, father of Jay Wolke, is a consultant to the Spertus Institute of Jewish Studies in Chicago. He was president of the United Synagogue of America and the World Council of Conservative Synagogues, and has served on the board of governors of the Jewish Agency and the executive committee of the World Zionist Committee. For forty-five years he was the president and chief executive officer of a chain of Chicago clothing stores.